Stage Fright

SOPHIA CAMPBELL

Fulton Books
Meadville, PA

Published by Fulton Books 2022

ISBN 978-1-63985-790-6 (paperback)
ISBN 978-1-63985-791-3 (digital)

Printed in the United States of America

CHAPTER 1

Kira

"I can hear it now. Kira Dorsey, aspiring child actress," I said dreamily. "Famed for her role as Wendy in *Peter Pan*."

My sister Katelyn sighed and walked briskly ahead of me. "Would you just *shut up* about that stupid play? You know you're going to get the part, so stop babbling about it."

"I'm *not* babbling," I insisted, jogging to catch up to her. "I'm just expressing my self-confidence."

"Babbling or not, I'm not going to audition, no matter how much you want me to."

I groaned. Typical Katelyn.

Even though I was annoyed with her for refusing my generous offer, I did really love her. After all, she and I were twins—identical twins to be exact. We both had the same curly brown hair, doe-eyes, and lean body frame. It was cool having someone who looked just like you—it got us lots of attention for one thing. Hey, I'm not conceited, but a bit of attention never hurts anyone.

Of course, there are downsides to being identical twins—like when we get compared all the time wherever we go. *Kira is more outgoing. Katelyn is smarter. Kira gets lower grades.* It's not a competition, people! And then, of course, there are the kids who just call us *the twins* because they're too lazy to figure out who's who. Honestly, though, I can't blame them. Katelyn and I are so identical that sometimes even our own friends can't tell us apart.

We were walking to Pine Hills Academy as we usually did on normal Friday mornings, except today was anything *but* normal. After school was the auditions for the upper school's annual musical. Ever since I was little, I've been obsessed with the idea of performing in a play. Year after year, from kindergarten through fifth grade, I had sat smack in the middle of the audience in the auditorium, gazing longingly up at the actors. Last year's performance was *Beauty and the Beast*, and I had desperately wanted to be Belle.

This year, Mrs. Kerrington, the drama club director, selected *Peter Pan* to be our play. And naturally, I was super excited. Pirate ships! Tinker Bell! Captain Hook! All that jazz! It felt amazing to finally be eligible for the show. I planned to audition this afternoon, for the chief female role of—drumroll, please—Wendy!

I skipped along the sidewalk, letting my backpack bump against my shoulders. "I can't believe it's here! The auditions! Finally!" I squealed.

Katelyn sighed again. She's not really interested in plays or musicals or pretty much anything besides academics. Sure, she boasted the highest IQ in the school, but what good does that do you besides getting you straight As and making you the teacher's pet anyway.

But however, if you were like me, you got to have tons of friends and go to carnivals and audition for plays! And star in them!

As if reading my thoughts, Katelyn gave me a pointed look. "Watch out. Your head is getting bigger by the minute. Soon it's going to be bigger than your mouth!"

"Rude," I flashed. The leaves crunched under my worn-out boots, and the sound was crisp and sharp in the silence.

Katelyn had a distant look in her eyes and didn't answer. I stifled a laugh. I knew what she was thinking about: the annual schoolwide trivia tournament!

Pine Hills had held the ultimate brainiac battle since pretty much forever, and Katelyn had been dying to compete for almost as long as I had been dying to be in the play. And like the play, you had to be in sixth grade to qualify. Basically, a bunch of smart alecks join up and are asked impossible (and useless) questions like: *What is the definition of abnegation?* and *The city of Baghdad lies along what river?*

4

Genius stuff like that. And for some reason, this is what Katelyn was interested in. Hey, I don't doubt she could blow all the other contestants out of the water. In fact, if I had to bet, my money would be on her, but I just don't understand why anybody would care to know the cube root of sixty-seven. I, personally, thought it was showing off. *Oh, look at me, my IQ is 275!* If you want to boast, join the drama club and do something productive with your time.

I could see our school up ahead on the block. I turned to Katelyn. "This is your last chance. You sure you don't want to be in the musical?"

I'd been trying to get her to audition for weeks. I wasn't forcing it on her or anything, I was only trying to improve her social life (something she seriously needed help with).

She shook her head firmly. "Oh, I'm sure. Academics are more important than after-school activities."

I stuck out my bottom lip. "It isn't an *activity*."

"Oh my gosh, you're so stubborn. Anyway, the show is on the same day as the trivia tournament, and I *can't* miss it."

I exhaled. It wasn't really worth trying anyway. Katelyn had her heart set on the trivia competition and didn't care for the play. Why my twin sister would choose boring hours of being asked useless egghead questions over the excitement and buzz of being on stage, I have no idea.

Together, we entered the school grounds, the March sunshine cool and sweet. There was so much going on. Students running to meet their friends, teachers trying to control the crowd, and stray backpacks left at random places in the schoolyard.

I adjusted my posture and held my chin high. Today was *my* day.

Weaving our way through the throngs of chattering students, Katelyn and I managed to make it down the hall, and sure enough, tacked to the door of every locker was an audition flyer for *Peter Pan*.

I ripped mine off my locker, clutched it to my chest, and danced around. I didn't care who was staring at me. The auditions were *today*! TODAY!

I felt a sharp slap on the shoulder. "Quit it," Katelyn hissed. "People are eyeballing you. They're going to think that you're me!"

Oh yeah! That was the thing about being twins. We always knew who was who, but other people—not so much. We were exactly alike, except for our harshly contrasting personalities and mannerisms. Still, we often got mixed up, although I couldn't understand why. I mean, there was fun, bouncy me, resident nice girl and knowing all the latest celebrity gossip. Then there was drab, lifeless Katelyn in a wrinkled T-shirt and baggy jeans. Huge difference.

Katelyn sighed and ignored the flyer taped to the door of her locker, which is next to mine. Without so much as a glance at the audition form, she opened up her locker. There's another difference between us—Katelyn's locker is four bare metal walls and nothing in it but dusty textbooks. It practically took all of my willpower to convince her to buy a shelf to stack her stuff on.

By contrast, mine was decorated with a magnetic pencil holder, a mini chandelier light, and a mirror, not to mention the pink floral wallpaper that I'd pasted around. Was it over the top? A little. But was it totally awesome and useful? Yes!

After I transferred my books from my backpack to my locker, I took a deep breath and faced Katelyn.

"See you at lunch."

We set off on our separate ways. I headed off to English class, a cool grin on my face, while Katelyn sauntered down to advanced math.

CHAPTER 2

Katelyn

My sister isn't stupid, but she's not exactly Albert Einstein.

Always and forever, I have been regarded as the "smarter twin." The twin with the higher grade point average. The twin with the honors roll certificates on her bedside table. The twin assigned to the advanced classes. (Yes, you can clap.)

Kira, on the other hand, struggles with even the most elementary of academic topics. If she heard me say that, she would either kick me or tell me I was talking like a college graduate, but I'm telling the truth! She finds it challenging to spell such words as *pharaoh* and *pterodactyl*. I've known how to spell those words since second grade.

Sometimes I feel bad for her like when I come home with a flawless report card, and she comes home with one that is, well, *flawed*. For some reason, she doesn't seem to care. I don't understand. How could you not care about something as important as your grades?

My first class was advanced math, room 109 near the end of the building. I had planned to arrive before the bell rang so I could snatch the center seat in the front row. I had heard we were changing seats today, so it was vital that I get this one.

I thought of the trivia tournament and relaxed. The tournament was to be held the same day and time as Kira's play, so while she would be singing on a stage, I'd be competing against some of the smartest kids in the school for the title of this year's winner. And oh boy, I knew I could win if I tried hard enough! Sure, I was only in sixth grade and would be competing against seventh and eighth graders, but I was smart. Really smart. I'd have tough competition, but I've competed in other stuff in the past—and crushed everyone else. So let the best brain win!

I found my classroom and quietly opened the door. I nodded a greeting to our teacher, Mr. Clark, and headed toward my selected desk. Only, somebody was there first—Eleanore Anderson.

I gritted my teeth. Eleanore was my greatest competitor and my worst nemesis. She had silky cocoa-colored hair that cascaded along her shoulders and dark eyes that knew a competitor when they saw one. She was almost as smart as me and twice as spiteful as she was smart. Last year in the fifth-grade spelling bee, her mother mouthed answers to her from the audience when she didn't know them. And the year before that, at the science fair, she copied my project and turned it in first so *I* would look like a poseur. Of course, she was never caught nor punished on either of those occasions.

And here she was, stealing the desk I had so desperately desired. The front-and-center seat. *My* seat.

I summoned the courage to confront Eleanore. Approaching her (my) desk, I eyed her cautiously and said as casually as possible, "You can't take that seat."

Eleanore had a smug little grin playing on her lips. She knew exactly what she was doing. "Why ever not, Kelly?" she said, her voice laced with sarcasm.

"It's Katelyn," I spat.

"You didn't answer my question," she sneered. "Why can't I, Eleanore Anderson, sit here?"

I couldn't answer that. There was no rational reason why I should take that seat. Eleanore had been there first, and I was second. I couldn't argue.

I pursed my lips, and Eleanore saw my annoyed expression. "Nothing? I don't blame you. With a brain like yours, I'm surprised you're even in the *advanced* classes."

My cheeks reddened. Was she, a less intelligent being than I, *insulting* me? Mr. Clark was still at his desk, shuffling papers. I didn't want him to get involved anyway, so I tried to conjure up a comeback of my own, but I was tongue-tied, at a loss for words.

Eleanore noticed my panicked expression and continued talking smoothly, "And do you recall me winning the spelling bee last year?"

"By cheating."

"Don't you dare tell anyone that!" she snapped, her face paling. "You'll ruin my exemplary academic record. Besides, I won the science fair before that too.

"You copied my project."

"Did not."

"Did too."

Eleanore sighed. "Well, anyway, *I* had this seat first, so *I* deserve it."

Not with that attitude, you don't, I wanted to say, but I kept my mouth shut. Let her have the glory. Let her be the first to get called on. I couldn't care less.

Couldn't care less? Yeah, right.

My thoughts were interrupted when, right at that moment, the door burst open, and students flooded the room. In a flash, all twenty-five desks were taken, leaving only one at the back-right corner. I stood uncomfortably in the front of the room. I didn't want to sit in that seat! The teacher would *never* see me from there! I craned my neck looking for another desk, but there wasn't one.

Eleanore gazed at me, her expression full of fake sympathy. "Sorry, Kayla. Isn't it such a *shame* you have to sit in the very back of the room? Such a tragedy," she murmured, quiet enough for only me to hear. Her tone was so infuriating! I knew I shouldn't be so offended, but I could feel my temper rising anyway.

My eyes flashed. "I won't."

"Well, where else do you think you're going to sit?" She laughed. "Twenty-six students minus twenty-five desks equals one desk. Sorry, honey, but there's nowhere else to sit." Her lips curled into a smile.

"Stop it!" I yelled angrily. I didn't care that I wasn't being logical. I wouldn't let Eleanore win again, but even I could tell that the words coming out of my mouth were pitiful. "You're a horrible, stinking, idiotic desk-stealer and I—"

"*Katelyn Dorsey!*"

I shut my mouth. Twenty-five pairs of eyes burned a hole through my back, the room in pin-drop silence. My heart dropped to my shoes. I turned begrudgingly to face Mr. Clark, his face red, his hands balled into fists. "What do you *think* you are *doing*, Katelyn?" he thundered.

I gulped. *Oh, crud. Now I'm in for it.* "Well, sir, I—"

"Well, nothing." He cut me off. "I will *not* tolerate shouting in my classroom."

"But Eleanore was—"

"I don't care what Eleanore was doing. You need to get yourself together."

With that, he whipped a little pink pad out of his pocket and wrote something on it. It was a detention slip.

My eyes widened. I'd seen teachers hand loads of kids those little pink slips, even Kira sometimes got one. But me, Katelyn Dorsey, labeled a bad kid? I couldn't believe it. I'd been trying so hard to be a good student, and here I was being sent to jail with my hands tied behind my back. Detention was for the troublemakers. I was anything but a troublemaker.

What made it worse was that, with a detention, I would be kicked out of the honors roll!

Mr. Clark pointed to the last remaining desk, the one in the corner of the room. "Sit," he commanded.

I walked over to the desk and sat.

Mr. Clark sighed. "Well, that's enough disruption for one day. Everyone, please take out your exercise book and complete problems one to fourteen."

I dutifully did as I was asked, but when we went over the problems as a class, Mr. Clark didn't call on me. Not once, even when I was waving my hand sky-high in the air. Obviously, I was on the blacklist.

The period passed in a blink. While everyone was packing up, Mr. Clark caught my eye and motioned for me to come over to his desk. Oh, gosh. What could he possibly want now?

Standing there in front of him, I suddenly felt exposed. I shifted uneasily. *What was he going to do, give me a year's worth of detentions? Kick me out from the advanced classes once and for all? Gosh, I hope not.*

I noticed Mr. Clark had concern in his eyes, and I felt a bit taken aback. But before I could consider what he was about to do, he cleared his throat and spoke in a low voice.

"Katelyn, I noticed you had a bit of a, shall we say, *meltdown* today, and I wanted to know if everything was okay."

Meltdown! Did Mr. Clark think that I was turning into some kind of bad kid?

"Oh no, sir, definitely not." I stumbled over my words. "I'm totally fine—it wasn't a meltdown—"

"Katelyn. I know you're a smart girl and would never dream of getting into trouble, which is why I'm going to make a deal with you. Hand over the detention slip."

I fished it out of my pocket and handed it to him then watched with wide eyes as he crumpled it into a ball and tossed it into the wastebasket.

"I think that socializing a bit more would do you good. You've been focusing far too much on school lately, and I think you should try something more social for once."

I bit my lip. *Social?*

He went on. "We have a fantastic drama club director and crew, and with a new play coming up, I think you should audition for it. I believe it's called *Peter Pan.*"

"*Peter Pan?*" I asked incredulously. "But I can't act!"

Mr. Clark arched an eyebrow. "Well, I think it's a great opportunity for you. You should get to know people."

I felt dizzy. "You mean if I auditioned for the play, you'll take away my detention?"

"Precisely." He smiled.

I groaned inwardly. I would be ejected from the honors roll if I had any detentions at all, but I could barely stomach the idea of performing on stage in front of the entire school. It was a lose-lose situation!

I tried to compromise. "How about I write the script? I'm good at things like that, you know."

"I think you'd prefer acting," Mr. Clark said.

I stared at him. "I don't mean to be rude, but what good could I possibly get out of this play?"

"It'll help you to lose the iron grip you've got on being a perfect student all the time." Mr. Clark gave me a tight-lipped smile. "Why don't you just audition after school today, and we'll see how it goes?"

He let me go after that. Even after consoling myself, butterflies were flying up a storm in my gut.

CHAPTER 3

Kira

Second period! One period closer to the final bell! One period closer to the auditions!

Katelyn didn't talk to me when we met at our lockers between first and second period, which barely concerned me. She's usually like this before a test or competition of some sort, and I knew she was probably stressed from the pressure of the trivia tournament.

I smoothed down my shirt and strolled confidently down to second period—history. English class had been a breeze since we were only working on pronouns and antecedents. Probably because I was in a lower-level class than Katelyn. Oh well, there were worse things.

I strutted through the hall, waving hi to kids I knew and even a few I didn't. I've done a ton of clubs over the years: cheerleading, dance club, cross-country, and more. The only one that's really stuck is drama club though. It just seems so exciting to perform in front of an audience. Now I might finally get my chance!

As I walked, I was secretly watching for anyone who was holding an audition flyer for *Peter Pan*. They were my competition, and I needed to be ready for them. As I was walking, I heard someone say, "Musical," and I craned my neck to look for them. Admittedly, this was a mistake because, in no less than two seconds, I slammed into someone, and we both tumbled to the floor, our books scattered.

I sat up and glared at the person who had just knocked me over. "Hey! What do you think you're—" then I stopped. The girl had straight chocolate-brown hair knotted into a French braid, and I burst out laughing. This wasn't any random kid, it was Abby!

Abigail Kent was my best friend. She was fun and daring and didn't care what people thought of her. She was smart too, not book smart like Katelyn but people smart.

"Kira! You dork!" Abby untangled herself from our mess of notebooks and backpacks. "You just nearly plowed me over!"

I grinned. "You mean, *you* just plowed me over!" We scraped up all of our scattered books and papers into a big pile and picked out which was ours and which was the other's.

"Look at this mess!" Somebody gave a tinkly laugh. I knew without looking that it was Yumiko and her two cronies, Alicia and Cheyenne.

Yumiko was the most annoying girl I'd ever met. For some reason, she liked to pick on me for absolutely every little thing I did. She provided (and created) local gossip, much of which was conjured up about the Dorsey twins. Naturally, both Abby and I hated their guts.

I brushed off my knees and stood up. Abby came up defensively behind me. "Why do you care what we do?"

Yumiko brushed her inky sheet of hair off her shoulders, which, by the way, was dyed a flaming scarlet at the ends. "Because you're in my way. If I had crashed into you two gremlins like you did to each other, I could've gotten injured."

Abby snorted. "Gotten injured? From what, hitting the floor?"

Yumiko sniffed. "Well, that explains why you both look like a hurricane hit you. One of you is going to end up with a black eye if you continue crashing around like that."

"You seem to care a whole lot about appearances," I retorted, "especially for someone who's *only* pretty on the outside."

"Why don't you just leave us alone?" Abby said flatly. "We're just minding our own business, and *you* barged in here like you own the place."

Yumiko's eyes narrowed. I glanced at her hand and stifled a gasp. Crumpled up in her palm was a flyer for *Peter Pan*, so Yumiko was going to audition!

This was a problem. Mrs. Kerrington, the drama club director, adored Yumiko because she was a great actress and seriously talented. I'll admit it, she would look fantastic as Wendy.

Yumiko noticed me staring, and a slow grin crept across her face. "Oh, you're going to audition too?"

I glanced nervously at Abby. "Yeah, and?"

"Both of you?"

I looked at Abby again. Abby was a magnificent artist and was part of the set designing crew backstage. She wasn't auditioning for the actual play though.

Abby pursed her lips. "Actually, no, I'm not."

Yumiko tossed back her head and laughed. "Oh yeah, you're working on the set. Let's just hope it's not as bad as it was *last* year!"

"Hey!" Abby said defensively. "The set was phenomenal last year!"

"If you call a couple of cardboard trees and rocks phenomenal." Yumiko sniffed.

I scowled. "Yumiko, I don't care. I'm going to audition, and you can deal with it."

Alicia, the sidekick, nudged Yumiko. "Do you think they're good enough for Wendy?"

"Not a chance!" Yumiko barked, though her statement and the expression on her face didn't match up. Was she intimidated? I choked back a laugh.

Abby threw her hands up in annoyance. "Kira, let's go. We're super late for history!"

I looked around. Yumiko, Alicia, and Cheyenne were departing in their own direction. I brought out my cell phone to check the time. Oh boy. We had been so carried away with talking to Yumiko that we were five whole minutes late for second period. Our teacher was *not* going to be happy.

But just as I was about to shut off my phone, it dinged with a text from Katelyn. It completely distracted me as I walked to class with Abby. I stared at the message mesmerized and realized that things were about to get complicated.

The message said: *Your wish has been granted. I have to audition for the play. Talk at lunch.*

CHAPTER 4

Katelyn

After shooting a quick text to Kira, asking her to meet me at lunch, I tried to focus on my classes, but focusing was impossible.

I felt like the earth had just reversed its rotation. I was now left with no choice but to audition for *Peter Pan*, the dreaded musical I had been painfully avoiding and something Kira had been trying to convince me to do for ages.

I'll let you in on a secret. Smart as I am, I have *glossophobia*—severe stage fright. I avoid publicly performing at all costs except when it's a competition.

For some reason, I feel a whole lot more comfortable when I'm competing in a spelling bee or a geography contest, whether it's on a stage or not. Answering questions just comes naturally to me. I know Kira thinks it's stupid and that I'm just a know-it-all, but I'd choose math over musicals in a second.

The first half of the day passed in a blur. School is usually very easy for me, but I've never felt this distracted before. I had an English quiz, and even though I'd been studying for it, I wasn't half as concentrated as I usually was. Most of the time, my mind kept drifting off to Neverland.

When the bell rang for lunch, I sought out Kira in the cafeteria. She was in the lunch line with her best friend Abby, holding a packet of Cheetos and talking a mile a minute. I grabbed her by the arm and yanked her out of the line so fast that she almost fell on top of me.

"Geez!" she shrieked. "What the heck is going on? I haven't paid for these chips yet!"

I dragged her over to the corner of the lunchroom. I looked around to make sure nobody was watching. "You got my text, didn't you?"

"Yeah—" Kira crossed her arms, awaiting my response.

I took a deep breath. "Well, you see, I have to perform in the musical." I poured out the whole story: how Eleanore stole my seat, how Mr. Clark yelled at me, and how he talked me into auditioning for *Peter Pan*.

I was breathless when I finished and glad to have somebody else talk for a bit. Kira had been surprisingly calm throughout my story, which is shocking.

Of course, I spoke too soon. For a few seconds, she eyed me intently, and then doubled over laughing.

"You're *actually* auditioning for *Peter Pan*?" she squawked, gulping for air. "I thought...I thought that was the *last* thing in the world you wanted to do."

"Yes, I'm auditioning," I stated, crossing my arms. "Got a problem with that?"

"No, but, I mean—you? Trying out for a *play*?" Kira dissolved into laughter again. I scowled.

I glared at my shoelaces and tried to keep my mind off the prospect of me singing and dancing on a stage. "It's not funny. I thought you *wanted* me to be in the musical. Remember that huge deal you made about trying to convince me to audition?"

"Well, yes, I *do* want you to audition, but I thought that was never gonna happen." Kira snorted. She stuffed another chip in her mouth. "But now you have to!"

I groaned. "Um, yes, but you know how bad I am on stage."

Kira's eyes bulged. "Yeah, I think *everyone* knows how bad you are on stage." She started laughing again, and I almost gave up talking to her.

I sighed and waited until my sister had calmed down. "Are you going to help me or not? I really don't want to audition. You know that. So I need some advice on how to perform!"

"Okay, okay, fine," Kira muttered. "Advice? All I can tell you is to do your best with what you've got. And since you're not naturally confident, just act like nobody's watching."

"How could I possibly do that in front of so many people?" I gazed across the cafeteria at all the other kids peacefully eating their lunches while Kira and I were over here panicking about *Peter Pan*. Suddenly, a thought occurred to me. I bolted upright and slapped my hand over my mouth. "Oh my gosh!" I cried.

"What?" my twin asked. She raised an eyebrow.

"The trivia tournament!" I exclaimed, beginning to pace. "It's on the same day as *Peter Pan*! I won't be able to be in both!"

Kira crunched into her apple. "So what? You can just go straight from the musical to the tournament. No big deal."

"It *is* a big deal!" I howled, clawing at my face. "They're at the *same time!*"

"Katelyn, Katelyn, chill. You're making a scene," Kira whispered urgently. Yes, people were staring at me. A lot of people. I lowered my voice self-consciously.

I crossed my arms. "But, Kira, if I don't perform in *Peter Pan*, I'll have to accept Mr. Clark's detention and be kicked out of the honors roll! But if I *do* perform, I won't get to compete in the trivia tournament!"

This was a huge problem. Whether I was competing or not, Eleanore Anderson was going to. I knew Eleanore was smart enough to win the tournament, and without me there up against her, the questions would be a breeze. She would beat out every other kid. I would never hear the end of it, and I couldn't bear to see her win again. Not this time.

I wailed. Kira bit her lip. "Why don't you talk to Mr. Clark or something?"

I recoiled as if this thought horrified me (which it did). "And risk ruining my flawless reputation as a good, obedient student?"

"Haven't you already done that?" Kira pointed out. "What with the whole desk-stealing episode and all?"

"That was Eleanore's fault."

Kira thought for a moment. "Okay, try talking to the drama director, Mrs. Kerrington? Maybe she can get you out of this mess."

"No!" I snapped, my face paling. "No way am I going to confront *any* teachers."

Kira rolled her eyes. "Well, if you're going to shoot down all of my ideas, I'm not going to help you." She swiveled and began to walk away, but I grabbed her arm again.

"No!" I cried. "Look, you know I can't ask Mrs. Kerrington *or* Mr. Clark. He's already giving me a way out of detention, and I don't want to push my luck."

"Then what are you going to do?" Kira gestured to all the people in the cafeteria. "Maybe you should just go through with the audition. I promise it won't be as scary as you think. Tons of these kids are going to try out, so you're all in the same boat."

"That doesn't make it any less mortifying," I said.

CHAPTER 5

Kira

Admittedly, I spent the whole rest of the day thinking about Katelyn. She'd gotten herself into *quite* a situation. Of course, I wanted her to audition, but I wanted her to audition *successfully*. The last thing I desired was for her to get up on stage and faint or something.

The bell rang, dismissing all classes for the day. This was it! The auditions were finally here!

I jammed my homework into my backpack, slung it over my shoulder, and dashed joyfully out of my homeroom. I made a pit stop at my locker to deposit my books. While there, I took a few deep breaths and smoothed down my hair and clothes. I wanted to look confident, polished, and talented at the same time. First impressions meant everything to me, and I needed to charm Mrs. Kerrington with my professionalness, or professionism, whatever the word was. Katelyn would know.

My heart skipped a beat. I slowed to a stop as I entered the auditorium, thinking, *Won't Mrs. Kerrington be impressed when I turn up first!*

I made a sharp turn through the doors and skidded to a stop, frowning, because I was *not* the first person there. The first person there was Katelyn.

There she was, sitting on the stage, swinging and dangling her legs over the edge. She looked miserable, which I had expected, and appeared to be muttering words to herself aimlessly. *Answers for the trivia tournament, maybe,* I mused.

"Ahem." I tapped my foot impatiently. Katelyn looked up.

"Oh! It's—it's you," she stammered.

I put my hands on my hips, and she shifted uneasily. "Why are you here so early?" I said.

She shrugged. "I like being early, even for things I don't want to do."

Always the perfect student. I was about to say something else when I remembered that I was here to fight for the role of Wendy. Katelyn wasn't much competition, but she was still something, and I mustn't engage with her.

I slipped my backpack off my shoulders and plopped down on the opposite side of the stage, pointedly ignoring my sister. Whether this hurt her feelings or not, I didn't know, but I didn't have any time to dwell on it because our peace was interrupted.

I heard the doors open and close with a bang. It was the drama club director, Mrs. Kerrington. She looked like she sprinted from the teacher's lounge; she was panting so heavily.

When she caught her breath, she smiled. "Ah, it's none other than Kira and Katelyn Dorsey! The famous Pine Hills twins." Her eyes widened and sparkled. "Can you read each other's minds? You know, I befriended a pair of twins when I was your age, and they always—"

Yep, it was Mrs. Kerrington, all right. As dramatic and enthusiastic as ever. She continued chattering on and on about *twins* until she noticed my boredom and stopped talking.

Mrs. Kerrington might have a seriously bad case of a blabbermouth, but she's really a nice woman. I have drama club after school every Wednesday with her, and she's round and jolly, and her orangish hair is cut like a pixie's. She's my favorite teacher at Pine Hills and for a good reason! She never gives any detentions, thank goodness. Oh, and no homework either because she doesn't believe in "unnecessary squanderings of free time." She's excellent in teaching us how to act better, how to sing, and how to present ourselves on the stage. I try my best to impress her in my drama classes, and though I might not sing as well as Lindsey or dance as well as Cara, my acting is pristine and perfect.

"Well, how have you girls been doing?" Mrs. Kerrington smiled brightly. "Are you excited for the auditions?"

Her eyes skipped from me to my twin. Me, who was trembling with nerves and pumped with anticipation. And Katelyn, who was staring aimlessly off into the distance, a sorrowful expression on her face.

"I'm thrilled to finally be able to perform this year!" I said, making sure to flash her my best movie-star smile.

Mrs. Kerrington nodded in approval. "And how about you, Katelyn?"

My sister snapped out of her daydream. "Me? Am I—oh. Yes, I suppose I'm excited."

A funny look came over Mrs. Kerrington's face.

*****

Within the next five minutes, the rest of the auditioning kids gradually arrived at the auditorium. My heart quickened when I saw Yumiko enter with her friends Alicia and Cheyenne. Wait! No! I couldn't feel intimidated. I raised my chin slightly and gave all three vultures my best death stare. Much better.

I wondered if Katelyn sizes up her competitors before a competition. I was doing that right then, looking at the range of heights, ages, and personalities of the kids around me. One of them was going to be Wendy.

I also saw Abby passing through the mess of kids, presumably looking for me. I didn't expect this because she was in the set crew and wasn't due to be at the auditions. I met her eyes and waved her over.

"Hey, what brought you here?" I asked.

"To cheer you on, duh!" responded Abby. "I can't wait to see how the auditions go. I'm so excited!" she squealed, jumping and clicking her heels together. "Aren't you!"

"Of course, I am!" I giggled. "I mean, I've been waiting for this day all my life! And it's here! Right now!"

I took a shaky breath. I felt energized and electric like lightning was coursing through my veins at this very moment.

"I'm a bundle of nerves," Abby admitted. "I mean, I know I'm not performing, but everyone's relying on me to design a good set. For a fantasy story with pirate ships and fairies and magic? That's going to be a challenge."

"What are you talking about? You're great at artsy stuff!"

Suddenly, I didn't feel so good. I'm not sure why. Abby was talking, but everyone's voices were starting to swim together. Then with a pang, I remembered Katelyn was standing patiently next to me, as scared as ever, and here I was, acting like she didn't exist. I felt kinda bad.

Mrs. Kerrington cupped her hands and yelled over the excited crowd. When a teacher speaks, people listen.

"All right! You all have your audition number pinned to your shirts? Good! Well, as you all know, I am the drama club director. Welcome to the auditions for *Peter Pan*, the twenty-sixth annual play of Pine Hills Academy! I am honored to—"

And she went on and on and on. By my side, Abby said, "And the chatterbox is at it again." I swallowed my laughter.

Without thinking, I reached over to Katelyn and grasped her hand. It was clear she was nervous. I squeezed her palm, letting her know I was here. You can all give me my Oscar now for being the best twin sister in the history of—

Oops! Everyone was beginning to line up. Mrs. Kerrington liked to audition the biggest roles first, and I watched as a bunch of boys lined up to audition for Peter himself. They had to say a few lines and leap around the stage. They were all pretty decent, some better than others, some worse. Katelyn was too busy picking her nails to observe, but Abby was watching them all with fascination. It's weird how she was just as obsessed with acting as I am, but she'd rather work backstage in the crew than perform.

"Second star on the right and straight on till morning," one of the auditioning boys announced assertively. Jacob Thompson was his name; he was in drama club with me and a favorite of Mrs. Kerrington's. He could act, sing, and dance with a dynamic quality that most of the other boys didn't have. I can see he'd make a great Peter Pan, with his fists on his hips and Tinker Bell by his side. Just as I would make a great Wendy.

CHAPTER 6

"What's the smallest role I can get?" I whispered to Kira. She jumped, obviously not paying me any attention up until now.

"What?" she said. Actually, she didn't *say* it. She *growled* it.

"I said, what's the smallest female part that I can audition for?" I repeated. Kira was too focused on the auditions—and Abby—to talk to me apparently. I know I shouldn't mind too much; she's my sister after all, and she loves me, right?

I could see her run the entire *Peter Pan* cast of characters through her mind in a split second. "Oh, I don't know. Probably Mrs. Darling, Wendy's mother. Or maybe Nana, if you wouldn't mind being a dog."

"No, no, no," I shook my head quickly. I could hardly see myself as a fuzzy Newfoundland mutt. "Can't I be, like, an extra or something?"

Kira sighs. "Mrs. Kerrington doesn't really *do* extras. She believes everybody should have a big part, and nobody should be in the background."

"So that means that Mrs. Darling is my only option." I swallowed the lump in my throat.

"I guess." Kira looked around to make sure nobody was listening to us. "You know that even if you audition for Mrs. Darling, it's not a guaranteed spot. You can still get something else."

My heart almost stopped. "What do you mean?"

"I mean," explained my twin, "that's just because you're auditioning for Mrs. Darling doesn't mean you'll get that part. You could be assigned something else if Mrs. Kerrington sees fit to do so."

I whimper involuntarily. This was getting worse by the sentence.

"You mean I could get Tinker Bell? Or Nana? Or Captain Hook?" I wailed, horrified. Goodness! I couldn't *bear* having to stand up in front of hundreds of people and have to read a thousand lines of monologue!

"Uh-huh," Kira confirmed.

I clawed at my face. "Augh!" I cried. I kept my voice down, though, because Mrs. Kerrington was still auditioning kids for Peter, and I didn't want her to notice me.

"Well, you probably won't get Captain Hook," Kira said quickly. "He's a guy role, obviously. You should consider yourself lucky because you probably won't even get one of the star roles."

My face crumpled, even though this should have been good news. *Gee, thanks, Kira. Just what I wanted to hear, that I'm a terrible actress.*

She saw my injured expression and softened. "I didn't mean it like that, you know."

"But you did," I replied quietly.

"Well, maybe you could, like, fail your audition on purpose, or something!" Kira suggested desperately.

"How is that going to help?" I moaned.

"Maybe you won't get cast?" Kira guessed.

But I knew without saying that in Mrs. Kerrington's plays, *everybody* has a part.

I decided then and there not to speak to Kira. What she was saying was not helping me at all. I turned my head squarely back to the stage and didn't say another word.

But before I had time to settle down, Mrs. Kerrington dismissed all eleven boys that were trying out as Peter Pan and called up the girls who wanted to audition for Wendy; that meant Kira, of course. I knew my sister was petrified, but here she was strutting up on stage, an aura of calm surrounding her. She stepped into the back of the line. I knew her trick. *"Be the last audition and blow everyone away. They'll remember you, then."*

I wondered what she was thinking right then. Maybe she was nervous, but it didn't look possible! She looked as cool as a cucumber. Before *my* competitions, my heart is always pounding up a hurricane. Kira didn't even seem to be breaking a sweat in the midst of all those girls trying out for the part.

Without looking, I knew the first person in the line of auditionees was Yumiko, Kira's primary source of misery. I'd heard way too much about that girl's antics from Kira's crazy after-school rants. Sure enough, neither one of her minions, Cheyenne and Alicia, were in the line. I snorted. Yumiko was so insecure. She had probably ordered them *not* to audition for the same part she was auditioning for! I looked for Alicia and Cheyenne in the crowd of onlookers and found them shuffling around in the back of the room, only half paying attention to Yumiko. I turned my eyes back to the stage and noticed at once that it had become pin-drop silent. Mrs. Kerrington was starting the auditions.

Yumiko pranced to the center of the stage and parroted back the lines Mrs. Kerrington threw at her. She added emotion and a theatrical flair to them, and at once I could see she stood a good chance of beating out everyone else, even Kira.

"Oh, Peter! You'll come visit us again, won't you?" Yumiko's voice was plaintive and sorrowful, pleading with a nonexistent Peter Pan to return to the Darling children one day. "Surely you will! You must!"

Finally, Mrs. Kerrington instructed her to perform a snippet of Wendy's solo song. From Kira's endless chattering, I knew that some of the songs that were to be used in the audition had been emailed out beforehand so we could prepare. It was crystal clear that Yumiko had indeed been preparing and preparing well. Admittedly, she had a beautiful, clear voice, dominating every note with the perfect melody. I looked back at Kira who was still in line. She looked sick to her stomach.

I found myself clapping when Yumiko finished her solo. She was breathtaking, and as expected, Mrs. Kerrington adored her.

"Wonderful! Marvelous! Perfecto!" the drama director applauded. "Yumiko, you blew the roof off this auditorium! Thank you so much for that astounding rendition."

Yumiko beamed and gave a small curtsy. Then she swiveled on her high-tops and sashayed off the stage. It was infuriating to see this self-centered little brat gifted with amazing talents. *Grrr.* No wonder Kira doesn't like her!

Speaking of Kira, she appears to be about to throw up.

CHAPTER 7

Kira

It's already a disaster, and I haven't even performed yet.

I mean, I knew Yumiko would audition. I knew she would suck up to Mrs. Kerrington. Heck, I even knew her performance skills were top-tier. I just didn't think she would be *this* good.

I shivered, but it wasn't because I was cold. As Yumiko pranced off stage, she gave me *the look*. She knew she'd won the part already and wanted to rub every inch of it in my face. My dreams were crumbling away like sand through my fingers.

"Okay, Vera, you're up!" Mrs. Kerrington invited the next contestant to the middle of the stage, and the line shuffled forward a little. My heart dropped to my toes. I was getting closer to my certain death.

Mrs. Kerrington winked. "Show us what you've got, Vera."

I didn't know Vera very well. She was in the science club and great at memorizing things (like scripts). I was surprised another brainiac, besides Katelyn, would audition.

And one by one, Mrs. Kerrington sifted through the line of possible Wendys until she inevitably came to me. I flinched and scoured the crowd of watching pupils until I found Abby. She gave me an encouraging smile, instantly boosting my minuscule confidence.

"And now we have our final Wendy audition, Kira Dorsey," Mrs. Kerrington announced smoothly. I bit my lip nervously and bounced on my toes. *Oh my gosh. Oh my gosh. Oh my gosh.*

Once I was situated on center stage in front of Mrs. Kerrington, she folded her hands and read me a few lines to say.

I took a deep breath and began to speak. "But, Peter, we can't come with you. The little ones must sleep, especially Michael, you know." I tried to make my voice sound disappointed yet gentle, hoping it would be realistic enough to please Mrs. Kerrington.

Her eyebrows shot up in surprise. "Excellent reading, Kira."

The drama director threw another couple of lines at me, and I gave them my best shot. With luck—and a pinch of pixie dust—I could be considered for the role!

But my joy was short-lived because, right then, Mrs. Kerrington told me I'd have to sing the first verse and chorus of Wendy's solo. Oh boy. This was going to be rough.

Then I reminded myself, *Abby is cheering me on. Katelyn is cheering me on. Yumiko is not cheering me on, but that doesn't matter because I'm going to show her I'm a contender for Wendy.*

I sang.

I was no Ariana Grande, but even George Richardson who always sat in the back of the classroom scraping wax out of his ears knew I was pretty good. I didn't try to show off or overdo it or be too dramatic. I just sang as honestly and as purely as I could, crossing my fingers that it would be enough to impress Mrs. Kerrington.

My moment in the spotlight ended almost as quickly as it had started. The music stopped, my mouth snapped shut, and I found myself exiting the stage. Abby met me in the middle of the crowd of spectating students, breathless.

"Oh my gosh, Kira!" she squealed. "That was amazing!"

I blushed. "No, it wasn't."

"No, no, no, don't shoot yourself down like that." Abby crossed her arms sternly. "You were the best of all of them. By a mile."

I didn't totally believe her, but I was grateful for the compliments.

"When do I go on?" said a voice.

"Huh?" I swiveled around, confused. Oh, it was Katelyn, standing behind me. "When Mrs. Kerrington calls for Mrs. Darling, I guess."

My sister was bright red, sweaty, and biting her lip—three top signs of nervousness. I thanked my lucky stars that she hadn't fainted yet.

I threw Abby a meaningful glance. "Could you, um?"

She understood immediately what I meant and backed away into the crowd.

I turned to Katelyn, relieved for the small amount of privacy we'd been given. "Hey, Katy, you've gotta calm down. You can't go onto stage like this."

Katelyn looked like she was about to hyperventilate. "Calm down?" she shrieked. "How can I calm down when I'm about to die of embarrassment?"

"Shush," I hissed under my breath. "People are going to think you're crazy."

"Well, that's really encouraging," Katelyn jeered.

"I'm just trying to help you!" I said defensively.

"You're doing it wrong."

I threw my hands up, exasperated. "All I can tell you is try not to pass out on stage. You'll embarrass me."

"Embarrass *you*!"

But neither of us had time to say anything else when Mrs. Kerrington announced, "All auditioning for Mrs. Darling, the mother of Wendy and her brothers, please enter the stage."

Katelyn looked like she was about to faint. "C'mon!" I urged, shoving her toward the stage stairs. "Go. You have to go."

"But—" argued Katelyn.

I cut her off mid-sentence. "No. No buts, ands, or ifs. Just go."

And that was that: my sister stood on stage for the first time, at the head of the line of kids trying out for Mrs. Darling. She was literally quaking in her boots, holding the mic with trembling hands.

Mrs. Kerrington shuffled some papers. "Okay, Miss Dorsey, can you—wait a minute. Didn't you already audition?"

Giggles arose through the crowd. Katelyn turned red. Mrs. Kerrington must have thought she was *me*, coming to audition again!

"N-no, ma'am," Katelyn stuttered. "I'm *Katelyn* Dorsey. Kira is my twin."

She's mortified. *Bad start*, I thought.

Mrs. Kerrington smacked her forehead. "Oh, yes, I spoke to you earlier. Well, then, Katelyn, please repeat this line for me, 'It's time to go to sleep, children. Yes, John, you too.'"

Shakily, Katelyn repeated her. I winced. It was average.

Mrs. Kerrington frowned. She read Katelyn a few more lines, and my sister repeated them dutifully. I could tell she was gaining confidence. By the fourth line, I realized my sister was actually a *fantastic* actress! Maybe brains do amount to something. Katelyn managed to make her voice soft and sweet, appropriate for the character, and coordinated facial expressions with her lines. She even added body movements to her part! I'll admit, I was shocked.

Next came the singing. "Okay, Katelyn, could you now please sing Mrs. Darling's line?" Mrs. Kerrington instructed. Lucky for Katelyn, Mrs. Darling didn't have any solo singing; she would only sing as a part of a chorus.

Katelyn froze in her place. She wasn't prepared for this. Her mouth opened, but no sound escaped.

Mrs. Kerrington noticed her panic and came to the rescue. "Why don't you repeat after me?" she said gently and sang a few lines. She prompted Katelyn to do the same.

Wow! I had expected my twin to be tone-deaf, since I've never heard her sing in my entire life, but shockingly, she could carry a tune. She was a promising actress as well as a decent singer.

"Well!" Mrs. Kerrington's eyes were twinkling. "I certainly wasn't expecting that. Excellent acting and singing!"

After her audition, she bounded offstage toward me, beaming ear to ear. "Did I do that well?"

I high-fived her. "You bet." Then my smile faltered.

"What's wrong?" Katelyn asked anxiously.

"I thought you *didn't* want to be good so that Mrs. Kerrington would give you a bit part. Now that you've done so well, you might be upgraded to a larger role."

The color drained from her face as she realized what she'd done. "Oh no! I don't even *want* to do this stupid musical. And now I've gone and messed it up!"

"Don't worry!" I said. "It's still possible she'll cast you as Mrs. Darling!"

At this, Katelyn howled. "But what if she *doesn't* cast me as Mrs. Darling? What if she casts me in a bigger role? I don't *want* to have a bigger role!"

CHAPTER 8

Katelyn

It felt like a massive weight had been lifted off my shoulders when Kira and I finally made it home from school. I collapsed on the couch, letting my backpack slide off my shoulders and tried to forget the auditions. However, this proved to be a difficult task while Kira babbled on and on about them with Mom in the kitchen.

"How did the auditions go, Kira?" Mom asked while whipping up dinner on the stove.

"They went *amazing*!" Kira exclaimed. "Guess what, Mom! Katelyn auditioned!"

"Katelyn?" A look of confusion passed over my mother's face. "I didn't know she was into theater."

"I'm not!" I moaned from my sprawled position on the couch.

Mom looked at me quizzically. "Then why did you try out?"

Oh boy. I walked over to the kitchen counter, took a seat on a chair, and explained the whole story. "Well, it started when Eleanore Anderson, a pathetic excuse for an honors student who cheated at the spelling bee *and* the science fair, stole my desk in math class. Then I yelled at her just as much as she deserved and got detention. Then Mr. Clark said that he would take away my detention if I tried out for the play because I needed to do something more social. I had to accept because if I didn't, I would get kicked out of honors. And then, well…I auditioned."

Mom stared at me like I was insane. Then she shook her head.

"It's not that bad," Mom said slowly. "Drama club seems fun, and maybe Mr. Clark was right. It would do you good to participate in more social activities rather than studying all day."

I covered my ears with my hands and howled, "Don't remind me!"

Mom saw that she wasn't going to get anything out of me, so she turned to Kira. "Did you act well? Was Mrs. Kerrington pleased with your audition?"

"I hope so!" Kira laughed. "I sang as well as I could've, and I think my acting was up to standards. The only problem is Yumiko."

"That girl you've been telling me about?"

Kira nodded grimly. "She's my biggest competition, and it looks like she's going to get Wendy, and there's nothing I can do about it."

"You're a great actress, Kira," Mom said gently. "I'm sure you're one of Mrs. Kerrington's top picks."

"You think?"

"Yes, I really do. How did your audition go, Katelyn?"

At the exact same time that I grumbled, "Terribly," Kira shrieked, "Wonderfully!"

Our mother looked doubtfully from one sister to the next, her eyes twinkling with both amusement and confusion. "So Katelyn thinks her audition was terrible, but Kira thinks it wasn't?"

I turned to Kira, my eyes pleading for her to explain. Twin mind-reading skills would really come in handy right now.

Some kind of nonverbal understanding passed between us, and Kira turned to Mom. "Well, basically, the drama performance and the trivia tournament are on the same day at the same time. So Katelyn can only sign up for one, and she *has* to do drama because, otherwise, the nerd classes, I mean, the *honors roll* will dump her. And you know how, um…she's not great on stage?"

I tried not to show my embarrassment when Mom nodded. Am I really such a wimp?

Kira continued, "So Katelyn decided to botch her audition so she could get the smallest, least-humiliating part possible, but she ended up not botching it. She performed really well actually. You could tell Mrs. Kerrington was impressed. So now she might get the main part, and that could be pretty terrifying, especially for her."

I rested my head in my hands. This was becoming more of a disaster by the second.

Mom ruffled my hair. "I'm sure you'll be fine. Kira can help you get over your stage fright. Right, Kira?"

"Probably not," Kira said helpfully.

"But the trivia tournament!" I whimpered.

"There will be plenty of other tournaments to compete in."

"But, Mom!" I whined. "If I don't compete, Eleanore Anderson will win, and I can't let that happen!"

My mother shook her head. She just doesn't understand. "Honey, I really think this play will be a great opportunity for you to come out of your shell."

My shell? I'm not a hermit crab!

"Besides," Kira added, "you might not even get that big of a part. We could just be all worried over nothing."

I sighed. "Yes, I suppose you're right. But if there were a total of twenty-six girls auditioning, we could assume that the probability of me being Wendy is one in twenty-six if each girl had an equal chance. But since I was 'one of the best,' as you say, we can estimate that there is a 10–30 percent chance of—"

"All right, pack it up, rocket scientist," Kira interrupted. "All I know is that Mrs. Kerrington liked your act. Whatever happens, I promise you'll have fun."

I snorted. "Fun? How can I have fun whilst fainting from terror?"

"Trust me, you can do it," Kira assured me.

"How encouraging of you, Kira. I'm sure Katelyn will do just fine," Mom spoke slowly and firmly in a tone that said, "*This conversation is over.*"

I threw my hands up in despair. I could see I was getting nowhere in this argument and was about to retreat to my room when the house telephone suddenly rang.

Kira dove over and grabbed it, knocking over a few glasses and mugs in the process. "Yes?" she asked the caller breathlessly. It is at times like these that I start to believe my sister is insane.

I heard some muffled speaking from the phone.

Then a pause.

"Katelyn, it's Mr. Clark," Kira hissed. "He wants to talk to you."

Mr. Clark? What could he possibly have to say to me so long after school ended? I took the phone from Kira, my fingers trembling. I really hoped this wasn't about drama club.

"Yes, Mr. Clark?" I asked nervously. "How can I help you?"

"Well, Katelyn, Mrs. Kerrington spoke to me earlier today," said Mr. Clark's voice from within the phone. My heart dropped to my shoes. "She said that she didn't expect you to be such a great live performer! She loved your audition!"

"Oh no!" I yelped.

Mr. Clark was confused. "What do you mean? Aren't you happy?"

"Yes, well, I suppose so, but I am *not* a live performer! I hate performing! Standing on a stage gives me the creeps."

Mom and Kira were watching me intently.

"Well, I find that quite interesting"—Mr. Clark chuckled—"because Mrs. Kerrington could not get enough of your acting! She said it was good enough for the cinema!"

I felt queasy. I didn't know what to say.

"Katelyn? Are you there?"

"Yes, sir."

"What do you think?"

"I think I can't do this."

"You most certainly can do it. I've faced many students just like you over the years."

"You have?"

"Yes, I have. I'll be leaving you now. Don't forget to do your homework!"

And the line went silent.

No less than two seconds after the call ended, Kira began demanding information. "Well? What did he say? What did you talk about? Is it about drama club?"

"Stop attacking me," I said calmly, turning my face away from her.

"I am *not* attacking you. Now tell me what you talked about!"

"We talked about Mrs. Kerrington."

"Be specific!" Kira commanded.

"We talked about…something Mrs. Kerrington said."

"Details!"

I groaned. "Basically, your lovely drama club director thinks my acting is just wonderful. So wonderful, in fact, that she specifically mentioned it to Mr. Clark who proceeded to call me just now. So it looks like I'm probably *not* going to play Mrs. Darling anytime soon."

"Don't worry," Kira said. "You still probably won't get one of the super main characters since Mr. Clark and Mrs. Kerrington know how squeamish you are about that."

I cringed. "I really hope so. I just can't see myself starring in a musical, singing and dancing and all that."

"I can't see you doing that either," Kira said without a hint of irony.

"Hey!"

"All right, girls, I think that's enough for today," Mom interrupted us. "Dinner is ready, and you need to eat. Katelyn, I'm sure everything is going to work out fine."

I sighed. For now, I'd just have to cross my fingers.

CHAPTER 9

I honestly can't understand my sister. Gosh! If Mrs. Kerrington had been that impressed with *my* audition, I'd be over the moon. When I close my eyes, I can vividly imagine Mrs. Kerrington jabbering every detail of Katelyn's audition to Mr. Clark. And then the image of Mr. Clark being so pleased that he decided to ring up our house at seven o'clock at night. It's not like I'm jealous or anything, but Katelyn should be astounded that *two teachers* were *this* impressed with her. Yet somehow my twin takes it as a personal offense. She only seems to care when the science teacher hands her yet another exemplary test score or when the English teacher praises her essays. Don't get me wrong, those things are great too, but the arts are where it's at.

And how could you possibly be afraid of performing? Performing is thrilling! Compelling! Electrifying! Not scary at all! I mean, I get it if you feel the heebie-jeebies before you go on stage. But to be so afraid of acting that you can't stand the thought of it? Now *that* I can't comprehend.

It was Monday morning, three days after the auditions, and the cast list was set to come out today. Over the weekend, I had annoyed my mother and sister to no end with my incessant chattering about the auditions. I'm sure they were relieved the day had finally come. I knew I was. I had been tempted to email Mrs. Kerrington and try to squeeze some of the casting details out of her, but Katelyn convinced me it wasn't a good idea. I guess it wasn't. But it didn't matter now because, in less than an hour, I was going to find out!

I shoveled cereal into my mouth faster than ever before, though I was careful not to get any on my shirt. Today was the day I would find out if I was Wendy or not, and I had to look presentable.

"Chill out," said Katelyn from across the breakfast table. "You're acting like you might never see food again."

"I might not."

"Oh, stop being silly," Katelyn scolded. "I don't know why you're so excited about this. It's just a little play."

My spoon fell out of my hand and landed with a *clang* on the table. "It is *not*. Besides, I could say the same about the trivia tournament."

"Sure you could, but I'm not the one eating like a wild beast right now."

"Fine." I backed up my chair and stood up abruptly and cleared off my side of the table. Then I dashed over to the door, slung my backpack over my shoulder, and was halfway down the driveway when I realized I couldn't leave without Katelyn.

I turned a full 180 degrees and sprinted back into the house, breathless when I skidded to a stop in the kitchen. "Katelyn!" I screeched. "Hurry up!"

She was still leisurely chewing on a piece of toast as if she didn't have a care in the world. I watched in agony as she swallowed, took a big gulp of orange juice, wiped her mouth with a napkin, and then did it again while taking her sweet time.

"Katelyn!" I shrieked. "We have to leave for school."

"It is currently eight o'clock," she stated plainly. "It takes us about ten minutes to walk to our school, which officially starts at eight-forty-five. With that logic, we still have plenty of time."

"Aughhh!" I howled, clawing at my face. "If I have to wait *another second* to see that cast list, I seriously think I might die!"

"Patience is hardly a leading cause of death."

"I didn't mean it literally!"

Katelyn rolled her eyes. She stood up and brought her plate to the sink at the pace of a tortoise with a broken leg. Then she scrubbed it ever so slowly, and I could've sworn it took five whole minutes for her to put it into the dishwasher.

By the time she had her backpack over her shoulders, I was practically bursting out of my shoes.

We—scratch that—*I* skipped down the sidewalk without a care in the world; Katelyn trudging glumly behind me. It felt like Friday again. My head was ablaze with a light show of emotions ranging from panic to anticipation to worry. But mostly anticipation.

"Aren't you excited?" I asked Katelyn.

"No," she scoffed. "We've gone over this. I do not want to be in the musical."

"That's absurd."

She closed her eyes and sighed. "Kira, please. I'm trying to enjoy my last few minutes before the casting list comes out."

"You act like it's a death sentence!"

"It is!"

Silence.

I could hear the birds tweeting above us.

I recalled five years ago when I was around seven years old. It was Christmas morning, and my sister and I were feverishly unwrapping our presents. My aunt had bought me a karaoke set. Not just a silly plastic microphone but a set of speakers, an amplifier, a mic stand, and a couple of CDs. I remember jumping up and down when I got that gift. Guess what Katelyn got? A dictionary. My aunt gave Katelyn a *dictionary*. But for some reason, she seemed to like it! While I was messing around with my karaoke set, Katelyn sat quietly in the corner flipping through the pages of that book.

"Katelyn, come sing with me," I had asked.

"No," she had said. "Singing is dumb."

It's pretty much been this back-and-forth argument all the years since. Katelyn always declared education superior to all else, while I stubbornly insisted that performing takes the cake. It's so frustrating being identical twins with somebody who is *nothing* like you.

We turned a corner, and there stood Pine Hills in front of us. I felt like I was going to burst. I wanted to run, but I'd probably trip and scrape my knees, and that would really suck, especially on a day like today. So I tried to remain calm, cool, and collected as I ventured onto the campus, only vaguely aware of Katelyn tagging along behind me.

It seemed as if everyone else was just as enthusiastic about the casting as I was. Around me, kids were tearing through the yard like buffaloes racing to the double-door entrance of the school building. I wanted to let loose too, but I tried to maintain control of myself.

Waiting at the doors was Mrs. Kerrington herself dressed like a kaleidoscope dipped in a paint can. Her shirt was a purple-and-yellow Hawaiian print, her leggings looked as if a kindergartner colored them in, and her shoes were shiny pink military boots. As boisterous and animated as ever, I pounced on her.

"Mrs. Kerrington!" I said earnestly. "The cast list comes out today!"

She tossed her head back and laughed. "Your friend Abigail said the same thing to me! Well, it sure does come out today. You'll see the lists on the bulletin board in the main hallway."

I resisted the urge to sprint past her into the building. "I want to look at it so bad, but then again, a part of me doesn't want to look at it. You know?"

"I get you," Mrs. Kerrington said, nodding vigorously. "I felt the same way when I was in *my* middle school drama club."

I was about to respond when I felt a tap on my shoulder. Turning around, I saw a pale-faced Katelyn behind me. "Well, do you want to go in or not?"

I gazed longingly into the building. "Let's do it."

My tentative first steps into the school hastened into a light jog, and then a run, and then a full-on sprint. This was the moment of truth.

Chapter 10

Katelyn

Three days ago, I did something I never thought I'd do. I auditioned for *Peter Pan*.

It was a forced decision, of course, but what choice did I have? I couldn't stand the thought of being kicked out from honors. If I'd chosen that path, Eleanore would remind me of it every single time I took a breath. Plus, ruining your entire academic record with a detention was way worse than a little bit of humiliation on a stage. Education always comes first no matter what.

Enjoying the weekend had been a struggle, while Kira would *not shut up* about *Peter Pan*. Every third word out of her mouth was Wendy or Tinker Bell or something else twice as stupid. Today was Monday, the dreaded day when the cast list would be taped on the bulletin board by the school office. Of course, Kira was all bouncy and excited and not at all anxious.

The entire walk to school, Kira had kept bugging me. It was torture. The next few weeks were going to be torture, too, as I would have to rehearse for the musical. Rehearsing! When was I going to have time for homework? Rehearsals could last for hours. Hours of reading vacuous dialogue and prancing around with fairies and Lost Boys. For what? A short performance after a few weeks? It was fruitless.

I retraced my steps all the way to last Friday morning. What had led to this disastrous chain of events? I had crashed into that boy, which caused me to be late for math class. Eleanore Anderson had stolen my seat, and I had lost my temper. Mr. Clark gave me detention. I traded detention for drama club. And now we're here.

Standing at the entrance to Pine Hills Academy.

Kira ran in front of me through the hallway, eager to get to the cast list. I trailed behind her. "This musical is going to be the death of me," I complained.

Kira skipped on ahead of me. "Don't be such a downer. Anyway, I'm sure you'll get Mrs. Darling. She's the least important part, you know."

Way to boost my self-confidence, twin, I thought to myself. All the same, I really did hope I got Mrs. Darling. Learning lines would be easy; I have a photographic memory. It wasn't like Mrs. Darling had that many lines anyway—that is, if I ended up getting her character.

Kira grabbed ahold of my arm and squealed, "Oh my gosh! There's the bulletin board!"

And sure enough, there was a giant sheet of paper pinned to the board, reading *Peter Pan Cast List*. It was surrounded by a throng of students, and an array of whoops, groans, and cries erupted as they each read their assignments. Kira struggled to read over the top of all the heads, but I just shoved my way through the crowd so I could be face-to-face with the list.

I decided to read from the bottom up. It seemed like a slower and steadier way of doing things. Alicia was cast as Pirate #2, George Richardson as a Lost Boy, some girl named Jean as Nana, hmm. This was odd. I couldn't find my name. Maybe I'd been too bad to even get a role? But how could that be possible after Mr. Clark's call last night? Especially considering I had been forced to do this against my own will. I kept sifting through the list but found that the space next to Mrs. Darling did not have *Katelyn Dorsey* beside it.

My stomach churned, and my fists got clammy as I climbed the list. In the back of my mind, something told me that nightmares could come true too. And as every name, every character, every column disappeared, I was left with one.

There, at the top of the list, the name Wendy Darling stood in a row by itself. But across from it, typed in big bold letters, was another name. The name wasn't Kira's. It wasn't Yumiko's either. It was mine.

The last thing I remember was my heart pounding, and then everything went black.

*****

I blinked. Everything was way too bright like I was standing face-to-face with the sun.

As my eyes adjusted to the sudden light, I realized I was in the nurse's office laying in a cot. The air smelled of hand sanitizer. On my right side was a table of magazines. On my left was Kira.

"What happened?" I croaked. I searched my sister's face for answers as a lump formed in my throat. Why am I here, missing valuable class time? "Did I have a heart attack?"

Kira shook her head vigorously. "Nope, you fainted. Can't say I'm surprised."

My memory was starting to clear as loose threads tied themselves together. "So…what happened? The cast list came out, right?"

"Yes," Kira said shortly. "Can you remember which part you got?"

"I—" Things were still fuzzy in my memory. All I could recall was seeing my name at the top of the cast list, panicking, and crumpling to the floor. *Come on, Katelyn, think.* Roles. Which roles? A Lost Boy? No, I most certainly was not a Lost Boy. One of Captain Hook's pirates? Nope. Could I have been Wendy? Yes. That was it. The nightmarish blob of recent events came together like pieces in a jigsaw, and here I was lying on a cot in the nurse's office cast as Wendy Darling.

"I got Wendy," I croaked. "Actually?"

"Yes, *actually*," Kira snorts. "Don't get me wrong, I'd love to be able to cheer you on, but it's *my* part you stole."

Whoa.

"Look, I didn't mean to—" I began, but she cut me off.

"Whatever. It doesn't make it any better that I didn't even get a good part. I got one of the pirates, which is *not* what I wanted. I won't get any attention! I'll probably just dance around on a wooden boat in a couple of scenes."

I felt her gaze locked onto me as I took this in. "So you didn't get Wendy?"

Kira rolled her eyes. "Correct, I didn't get Wendy."

"You got a pirate, instead of Wendy, which was the part you very successfully auditioned for?"

She sighed and started talking to me like one would to a three-year-old. "Look, Katelyn, this isn't hard to understand. You're a genius, aren't you? I'm in no position to argue with Mrs. Kerrington, but I'm not exactly thrilled over my *twin sister* getting the role that *I* wanted. You're smart. So try to understand."

I let this sink in. Of course, Kira was jealous. I mean, I didn't even *want* to be in the stupid play, and I got the main part. Kira had been dreaming of getting a lead for years, but she only got cast as a pirate.

I moaned dejectedly. The nurse looked over at me from her desk. Everything was going wrong. "Kira, I'm so sorry. Maybe I can talk to Mrs. Kerrington and sort something out. You deserve Wendy way more than I do."

Kira gazed out of the window. "You can try," she said, "but Mrs. Kerrington doesn't let her mind be changed."

"Sure she will. Anyway, maybe I can quit. Mr. Clark only said I had to audition for the play, not actually perform in it. I'll just pretend to be sick, drop out, and my understudy can take my place. Easy."

"It's not that simple, Katelyn." Kira fiddled with her bracelet. "The problem is, well…you know Yumiko?"

"Yumiko? The girl you whine about every day after school?"

She laughed without humor. "Yeah, that one. Well, she's your understudy."

Oh no. An understudy was a person who would take the place of a lead if they happened to be sick or injured and couldn't perform.

"And I just can't bear seeing her get to be Wendy," Kira continued. "So…you have to do it. You have to do the play."

I seized a magazine from the side table and hurled across the room in despair. The nurse looked up again. "You okay, miss?"

I didn't reply. "But, Kira, you know I have stage fright. I just *can't* go out there. I can't. I'm sorry."

Kira swallowed hard. We haven't really been getting along lately, but we're still practically two halves of the same person. I felt a little bad about letting my own sister down and quickly changed my mind. I sat up in the cot.

"You know what? I'll do it. I *can* do it. I have to," I said.

Kira glanced at me sideways. "You're going to perform?"

"Yeah, I guess so."

Kira smiled, but it was a rather guilty kind of smile as if regretting being so fired up about the play. Hey, at least she knew how terrifying this was going to be for me. Mom said that she would coach me through my stage fright, but I can hardly see Kira doing that.

I was seriously scared about acting (and singing) on stage. And there was also the part about not getting to compete in the trivia tournament. Oh well. I'm sure I'll figure something out. Maybe I can ask the school board to postpone it.

But even though it sounded like a good idea, my heart was already telling me it wouldn't work.

CHAPTER 11

Kira

Okay, I'll admit it. I was being pretty mean.

Well, what was I supposed to do? Oh, here's a round of applause for Katelyn, my twin sister who got the lead role in *Peter Pan*. A role she would kill *not* to get. And on top of that, she got to sleep through the whole school day in the nurse's office.

At lunch, I had eaten with Abby, the only person who would *really* understand how I felt.

"What's up?" I had asked glumly as Abby slid into my unoccupied table.

"Not much. Hey, Kira, I'm really sorry you didn't get the part you wanted. You deserved it," Abby had said comfortingly.

I stuffed a chip into my mouth and pouted. "No, I didn't."

"Yes, you did."

"Mrs. Kerrington doesn't think so."

That had left Abby momentarily at a loss for words until she said uncertainly, "Maybe it'll be good for Katelyn."

"It will, I know it will"—I tilted my chin—"but she's terrified. She can't stomach even the thought of performing."

Abby looked up, searching for an answer as if one would be floating in the air. "Have you tried talking to her about it?"

I snorted. "She panics when I even mention it."

"How about telling Mrs. Kerrington?"

"Forget it."

"Couldn't your mom help her?"

"As if! Katelyn is impotent," I had announced dramatically. I wasn't really exaggerating, though, considering that just the word *musical* sends my sister into an unnecessary frenzy.

"Maybe I could help her," Abby had suggested thoughtfully. "I might be in the crew, but I know a thing or two about stage fright."

I shook my head. "Thanks for the offer, but I'm pretty sure Katelyn is beyond help." I had shrugged as if to say, "*What can you do?*" Because, honestly, what *can* you do with a person that would rather shave their eyebrows off than score the lead role in a show? What was she so afraid of? Katelyn had a photographic memory, so remembering lines wouldn't be a problem. I also now knew that she definitely had talent. So why was she so afraid of the stage?

I'd dumped my food tray into the garbage can as lunchtime came to a close and thanked Abby again.

And now, here I was, stuck in the nurse's office waiting for the school day to end. And end it did; the bell chimed at precisely 3:30 p.m.

Katelyn turned over in her cot. I slouched against the wall while the scent of expired hand sanitizer wafted through the room. The nurse hadn't once gotten up from her computer all the while I'd been here, which was since the end of last period. The only movement she'd made was when she'd turned to stare at Katelyn and me.

Katelyn, also known as Wendy.

Hmph.

I didn't have much time to think over this, though, because at that exact moment, the clinic door burst open.

It was our mother.

She was sweating and red in the face, and I could tell she'd sprinted here straight from work the second she'd heard of Katelyn's condition. Typical Mom. "Kira? Katelyn? Katelyn, honey, are you all right?"

My sister arose from the cot and smoothed down her wrinkled clothes. "Yeah, I'm fine."

Mom wasn't that gullible. "I heard you *fainted*! Why? Are you okay, honey?"

Katelyn opened her mouth to speak, but I interrupted her. "We'll tell you in the car," I said, not wanting to spend another second in this dump. Besides, I'd prefer *not* to have the nurse hear our sob story.

Once we had piled into the backseat of the Honda and cruised out of the carpool line, Mom demanded information. I let Katelyn explain it all.

"So you know that play Kira and I auditioned for? Anyway, the cast lists came out today, and Kira…didn't get the part she wanted. I got it instead. I got Wendy."

Mom hid her shock well. "That's fantastic, honey! Especially with your stage fright! I'm so proud of you."

I slumped against the car door and stared out the window. Mom's eyes drifted to the rearview mirror. "You okay back there, Kira?"

I mumbled a reply.

"What part did you get, honey?"

I said nothing.

"She's a pirate," Katelyn piped up helpfully. I gave her the death stare, but she wasn't paying attention to me.

"Well, that's fine, Kira," said Mom. "A pirate's a good part, you know."

"It is *not*!" I snapped. I knew I was being rude, but I just wasn't in the mood for conversation.

There was a painful pause while Mom decided what to say.

"Well, either way, honey," she said slowly, "I'm sure acting and rehearsing will be a great experience for you. And anyway, rejection is a big part of an actress's life."

"Well, I don't want to get rejected all the time," I sneered.

Mom's mouth flattened into a firm straight line. "Kira, come on. It's not *all the time*. This was only your first audition. Why don't you congratulate your sister on her success?"

"Congratulations, Katelyn," I said mechanically.

Mom sighed. I could tell she felt bad for me. "Look, I know how much this means to you, but for the time being, just keep a positive outlook. I'm sure things will turn out all right."

Oh, jeez. She sounds like one of those overly optimistic motivational speakers on TV.

"Did you see who else got a part?" interrupted Katelyn. I'd almost forgotten she was here in the seat next to me. "What did Jacob Thompson get?"

"Peter Pan, of course. He's good enough for Broadway," I answered without hesitation. "Nadia Coleman got Tiger Lily, and some girl named Vera got Tinker Bell."

Katelyn glanced at me briefly. "Vera? Vera Smith?"

"Um, yeah. That's what I said. Vera Smith as Tinker Bell."

My sister drummed her fingers on her lap. "Vera is in all the honors and advanced classes with me. I must admit, I'm surprised to find her getting a part."

I arched an eyebrow. "What do you mean?"

Katelyn sighed as Mom pulled onto our street. "Vera's not exactly performance material. Not that I've seen anyway."

"Hold up, hold up," I stopped her. "Since when do *you* know what performance material is?"

Katelyn glowered at me. "Well, I got Wendy, didn't I? Doesn't that make me a good judge?"

"You're just a geek, and Mrs. Kerrington gave you that part because she felt sorry for you," I retorted. Mom's eyes darted from the road to the rearview mirror and back again.

Katelyn sniffed. "What do *you* know anyway? You're a self-obsessed dork who whines like a baby when she doesn't get her way!"

"Oh yeah? Well—"

"Girls!"

We fell silent.

Mom sighed. "Will you two *ever* learn to stop arguing?"

Katelyn folded her arms and shifted to face the window. I toyed with a bracelet chain and gazed off into the distance.

I knew we didn't get along very well, but she was my twin, quite literally the other half of me. I found myself wishing we were better friends.

Wait! The dark corner of my brain hissed. *You don't want to be friends with a stuck-up, smart-aleck, big-headed nerd, do you!*

Shut up, I told it, but I still thought about it the whole day.

CHAPTER 12

Katelyn

After the miserable car ride from school, I expected the rest of the day to be just as depressing. But oh boy, was I wrong! Our dad, who had been on an endless business trip for the past few weeks, was there to greet us at our doorstep. He'd been at work in Europe for way too long, and it had been difficult to function at home without him. But here he was, making a surprise appearance with perfect timing!

"Hi, girls!" he shouted, opening his arms as Katelyn and I leaped out of the car and clamored to reach him.

"Dad!" I shrieked and engulfed him in a bear hug.

"How are my two favorite daughters?" He beamed. "Did the auditions go well? Your mother let me know you were *both* going to be in the play!"

"Not very well," I admitted.

"Not very well!" Kira screeched. "You got the star part!"

"I didn't want to!"

"Kira, Katelyn," Dad calmed us, his eyes twinkling. "Why don't I have your mother tell me about it?"

Mom ventured up from behind us and folded her arms. "Kira's unhappy that Katelyn was assigned the role of Wendy, though Kira wanted that part so desperately. Katelyn, however, did not want the part at all."

Dad appeared amused and nudged Kira playfully. "Oh, so we've got some jealousy going on here!"

Kira wrung her head guiltily. "I'm sorry, I can't help it."

Dad nodded then turned to me. "And you don't want this part, Wendy, but you had to take it due to a certain arrangement with your math professor?"

My cheeks burned with embarrassment. "Put simply, yes. I would greatly prefer to trade parts with Kira."

"That's not allowed," Kira stated the obvious.

"I *know* that." I rolled my eyes in annoyance. "I was just saying how I felt."

"Have you tried talking to Mrs. Kerrington about it?" Dad asked, speaking to both of us.

"No," we answered in unison.

"It won't work," I said.

"Mrs. Kerrington's pretty steadfast in her opinions," said Kira.

Dad looked thoughtful. "Well, then I guess this will be a learning experience for the both of you."

Kira squawked, "I hate learning!"

I squawked, "I love learning!" then quickly added, "but not if it's related to drama club."

*****

The next morning at school, I could feel everybody's eyes burning into my back like lasers. I felt like I was the subject of every whisper, every conversation, and every juicy tidbit of gossip. This isn't where I wanted to be. I longed to be back in the days when I was only the center of attention for winning the spelling bee or getting the highest grade on the geography assessment.

I was torn between drama and the trivia tournament. If I didn't do the play, I would be kicked out of honors. We've covered that already. But if I *did* do the play, I would miss out on the tournament and a chance to beat Eleanore once and for all. It was a dilemma.

I'd weighed every angle, every strategy, and every distant possibility, but there's just no escaping what I've brought upon myself. The worst part is that it's *my* fault. I don't have anyone to blame it on.

The mood this morning hadn't been any better than the day before. Kira was still miffed that she'd gotten a bit part, and I was shell-shocked from the whole fainting episode yesterday. Our walk to school had been cruel and silent, and Kira had sped past me the second we hit the campus. I was trying my best to maintain a sunny disposition, but it proved difficult as the atmosphere around me was so sorrowful.

As I slunk through the school halls, I heard somebody fall into step beside me. It was Kira. I said nothing.

She took a deep breath. "Katelyn, I'm sorry for being sour. It was unsportsmanlike."

"I don't want to hear it," I snapped. Kira shrank away from me, and instantly, I felt terrible.

Now it was my turn to take a deep breath. "Kira, it's me who should be sorry. I stole the role that you deserved. Mrs. Kerrington probably gave me Wendy because she felt bad for me, and I can ask her to change it or—"

"No, that won't work." Kira waved her hand dismissively. "Has a kid *ever* gotten Mrs. Kerrington to change her mind?"

She had a point.

"Rehearsals start today after school," she reminded me.

I grumbled, "Geez, they really get us working early, huh?"

"Mm-hmm."

"All for nothing because I don't even want this."

Kira smiled triumphantly as if she had already won the argument. "Hard work is good for you."

"You sound just like Mom," I moaned as my cell phone binged with an unwanted text. I decided I didn't have time for this.

"Sorry, Kira, but I have to go. I've got work to do in Mr. Clark's class. Can't be late."

I parted ways with my sister. As I wove through the halls to my classroom, I could almost hear Kira in my head mumbling, *Late, shmate. You're such a perfectionist.*

I remembered the text I got. I fished out my phone from my pocket and quickly checked it. It was from Eleanore Anderson. Why the heck was *she* texting me? I skimmed it quickly: *Too bad you're not going to compete in the trivia tournament, Kiara.*

I was so distracted by this message that I was still staring at my phone as I walked down the hall, mesmerized. And of course, I promptly tripped over my own feet. I landed in a miserable heap on the floor, my phone squashed under me, and I could hear the kids around me snickering. Eleanore laughed the loudest.

"What happened to *her*?"

"What a slob!"

I stood up, collected my mobile device, and dusted off my jeans. I turned to the laughing Eleanore and gave her a fixed stare.

She raised an eyebrow. "So you got my text?"

"You could've just said it to my face, you know. I was only a few meters away from you. But apparently, you're such a coward, you have to resort to electronic means to get your message across."

"Is that supposed to be an insult? Sounds pretty lame to me," Eleanore remarked. I blushed, not because of her but because I was painfully aware of the students who were hungrily watching this all go down. There were at least ten prowling silently around me like sharks.

"Why do you care what I do?" I blurted out.

"I care because you're a problem," Eleanore hissed, coming right up to my face.

"Is my intelligence a threat to you?"

"*No!*" Eleanore roared, louder than expected. "I meant, you're annoying, and you get in my way."

I shifted uncomfortably. "I, uh…I'd better get to class."

Eleanore's lips curled into a proud smile. "I'm going to win that tournament, Kadence."

"My name is Katelyn," I griped.

She marched away, unbothered, and the other kids departed with her. I sped off to Mr. Clark's room, shaking my head.

Once I arrived, I took my seat (in the back) as quickly and quietly as I could. I was still steaming from the hallway episode, but I couldn't let it distract me from the lesson.

Mr. Clark's chalk squeaked on the board, and I copied down everything he wrote as quickly as possible. It was easy stuff: percentages, decimals, fractions, the like.

I wondered what Kira was doing in lower math. Contrary to popular belief, I could *not* read my sister's mind, nor could I tell what she was doing at any given moment.

Twins are human beings too, people! We're not an exotic breed of alien.

*****

"I hate it already," I announced to Kira at lunch break. "Hate it! Hate it! Hate it!"

Kira took a massive bite of her peanut butter and jelly sandwich. "Hate what?"

I gritted my teeth. "The way people treat me. The stares I get. All because I'm Wendy. I *hate* being Wendy."

"Well, that's the surprise of the century!" Kira announced, sarcasm coating the edges of her voice. "Katelyn, people are going to stare at you. That's a given. You have the lead role, for goodness' sake. Plus, we haven't even started rehearsals yet. You're gonna need to toughen up quickly!"

I glared at my uneaten tray of food. "Where's your friend anyway? Abby, I mean."

"Home sick. Flu."

I glanced around the cafeteria. My eyes automatically fell upon Eleanore's table where she always sat with the rest of her little clan. The way she chose her friends was ridiculous; her criteria were essentially: (a) you must be smart, *but* (b) you can't try to beat her in any science fairs or anything. Sounded like a great little group to me.

Upon looking closer, I noticed that her army had formed a circle around her, and she was chattering wildly to them. I could hear laughing.

"Who are you staring at so weirdly?" Kira craned her neck to get a glance at Eleanore.

"I'm not staring weirdly," I said, flushing red.

"Yes, you are," Kira said, as stubborn as ever. "You looked like you had just sucked on a lemon."

I waved my hand. "It's nothing."

"It can't be nothing. It has to be something."

"Oh, Eleanore's just been getting on my nerves lately! That's it. Why are you so keen to know?" I squawked in exasperation.

CHAPTER 13

The walk from homeroom to the auditorium for rehearsal was a long one. I met up with Katelyn after the bell rang, and we set off for the auditorium together. I was already jittery for the first rehearsal, and it didn't help that Eleanore Anderson had decided to torment and stalk us on the way there.

"Going to rehearsal, huh?" Eleanore hollered from behind me in a singsong voice. "How *educational!*"

"Don't look at her," I hissed to Katelyn. Rehearsal started soon, so I picked up my pace. "She's not talking to you."

Katelyn gritted her teeth. "Yes, she is!"

"She's just trying to annoy us," I said, weighing the logic. "Get us off our game."

"There is no 'us'! She's after me!" snapped Katelyn. "Didn't you hear her? She thinks it's pathetic that I have to do this theater thing instead of the trivia tournament."

I was going to counter that statement when Eleanore confirmed my sister's fears.

"It's such a step-down," she snickered with fake sympathy, skipping down the hallway behind us. "I mean, who would've known you'd choose childish shenanigans over a contribution to your Harvard application?"

My hands balled themselves into fists, and my vision went red. Eleanore was cackling like the Wicked Witch of the West herself. Too bad we weren't performing *The Wizard of Oz.* I would've loved to see her melt into a puddle.

I was about to make a smart-mouthed reply when I heard a high-pitched voice from behind me.

"Eleanore Anderson! Do you want me to report you to the principal? Or would a detention slip suit you better?" On the delivering end of these fierce words was a blond shrimp of a girl with striking blue eyes and a yellow sash labeled Hall Monitor.

The weasel on the receiving end stuck her nose in the air. "You can't do anything! You're just a volunteer with no practical powers."

The blonde girl stepped forward, and I realized I recognized her from auditions. What was her name, Vivi? Veta?

"Aha! I know what you deserve!" the girl said. "A personal account to the school board for bullying!"

Eleanore swiveled around and stormed away without a word. Katelyn turned to the hall monitor, beaming.

"Vera!" she said with relief. "Thanks."

Ah, so this was the girl who scored Tinker Bell, I thought, glad to put a face to the name.

"No need to thank me," Vera said proudly. "It's the least I can do after you two had to deal with her."

Vera turned to me and stuck out her hand. I shook it gratefully.

"My name is Vera Smith," she announced. "And I'm assuming you're Kira Dorsey?"

"That's me," I said. "Congratulations on being cast as Tinker Bell! That's an amazing part."

"Thanks!" Vera exclaimed. "And congrats to you two as well! You're both amazing!"

I rolled my eyes. "Come on, I'm only Pirate #6. Katelyn's the amazing one."

Katelyn jabbed me with her elbow. "I just got lucky with Wendy. I definitely don't deserve that part." Then she sighed. "Gosh, I wish I could just do the trivia tournament and shut Eleanore up."

Vera cocked her head to the side. "Why are you so worried about Eleanore? You shouldn't care what she thinks."

Katelyn shuddered. "She scares me."

Vera shrugged and wrinkled her nose. "There's nothing scary about her. She's just a bully who knows that you're smarter than her and takes that as a personal offense"—she paused—"by the way, which one of you was the twin that took a nosedive to the floor before first period today? That looked pretty bad."

At precisely the same time that I shrieked, "Katelyn!"

My twin spluttered, "Kira!"

Vera squinted and looked us back and forth. "Umm?"

A few awkward seconds later, I thought I'd better clear things up. "It was definitely Ka—"

Katelyn slapped a hand over my mouth and dragged me away, an apologetic look on her face. "Sorry, Vera. See you at rehearsals! You won't be late, will you?"

"No, I'll catch up with you! Go before Kerrington flips her lid," Vera yelled as we departed.

CHAPTER 14

The time 3:41 p.m. officially marked the commencement of our first *Peter Pan* rehearsal. I strode into the auditorium. Whispers erupted from the kids around me as I walked in: Wendy this, Wendy that! Couldn't I just be known as Katelyn?

I quickly took a seat beside Kira in the front row of fold-up chairs. Mrs. Kerrington stood proudly upon the stage in front of us and clapped twice to gather everyone's attention. The whispers halted, and for once, I felt glad to have the spotlight stolen from me.

"Welcome, students!" Mrs. Kerrington boomed. "You lucky ones here have been selected to take part in the twenty-sixth annual drama production. I am exhilarated to produce yet another stunning play for the school!"

"If she does say so herself," Kira murmured. I jabbed her in the side, and she quieted without so much as a yelp.

"Currently in the art room across the hall is our crew! They will have a great deal of work preparing backdrops and props, so I expect you all to be at their beck and call."

A couple of kids groaned. Some seemed pleased. I shifted uneasily, realizing that, at some point, Mrs. Kerrington would call the leads up to the stage and introduce us. I shimmied farther down in my seat.

"As you may know, our leads for this performance"—I knew it—"are Jacob Thompson and Katelyn Dorsey as Peter and Wendy, respectively."

She beckoned for me to stand up, and I did. I made sure not to turn my head, afraid the kids around me would be laughing.

From behind me came a squawk of dissatisfaction as one kid made an unnecessary comment, "Why *her*? She's a nerd!"

Chuckles and nods of agreement erupted around me before Mrs. Kerrington could quiet everyone down. I collapsed back into my seat, wishing I could just disappear.

"Psst, Katy!" Kira handed me a towering stack of papers that was being passed down the rows of chairs. I took one and tossed the rest to the person behind me.

Mrs. Kerrington was still droning on, but her words faded into murkiness as I became lost in what I had just received: a fifty-page script. I flipped through it hastily. *Wendy* appeared next to the margin way too many times for my comfort, and I thanked my lucky stars I had a good brain to memorize all of these lines with.

"Please read over your scripts thoroughly and try to begin memorizing your lines," Mrs. Kerrington said, clasping her hands together. "We will be having rehearsals each afternoon leading up to the show, which will take place in exactly four weeks and two days. Rehearsals are mandatory with the only exception being life-threatening injury or death."

A familiar voice interrupted Mrs. Kerrington. "Ma'am, since there are two acts to the play, can't the understudies step in for one of them? The leads would be *so* tired."

Mrs. Kerrington looked uncomfortable. "Well, Yumiko, that's not quite how we run things. I believe you are Wendy's understudy?"

It was so quiet, you could hear a pin drop. I felt Mrs. Kerrington's gaze fall upon me.

"But, Mrs. Kerrington," Yumiko pleaded, "surely you can offer the understudies a chance to perform. We have to attend all the rehearsals anyway. It's so unfair!"

Mrs. Kerrington licked her lips then cleared her throat. "Unfortunately, that's not how an understudy works. Anyway—"

She kept talking, but I heard nothing. Wendy was given to me out of pity; some kind of teacher scheme that would "do me good." I knew deep down that I was no match for any of the other kids in this room. Mrs. Kerrington surely would've picked someone else over me if it hadn't been for me and Mr. Clark's run-in. I felt the way they all saw me: invisible, unwanted, and good for nothing at all.

And that's when I made my decision, sitting on the flimsy chair in the front row with my hands folded. I decided would put every ounce of my being into this role. I *would* play Wendy, and I would play her well. And I would show them all that Katelyn Dorsey is more than just a shadow of her identical twin sister!

*****

"Can you *please* stop doing *that?*" Kira's head dangled down over the side of her bunk bed.

I looked up at her and smirked. "What, exactly, is 'that'?"

Kira gestured feverishly to the neat stack of notecards I was shuffling and arranging. "I don't know, whatever you're doing with those cards. It's eleven o'clock, and you're keeping me awake."

I shrugged. "Does it matter?"

The Dorseys aren't night owls; it's uncommon for us to go to bed later than ten thirty. Kira will never sleep if she hears me making noise below her. Oh well, this is important. Sleep can wait.

"What are you even doing?" Kira's brown curls fluttered as she talked. "Something for school?"

"Wouldn't you like to know!" I scrunched myself farther under my bed covers. I was exhausted from this afternoon's rehearsal. We spent much of the time reading through our scripts individually to prepare for tomorrow's read-through. Mrs. Kerrington had basically said we'd be performing the entire play, without blocking or singing any of the songs, using our scripts. It's supposed to help us to get a better idea of the plot before we take a deeper dive into stage placement, acting, and the musical aspect of the show. I knew that if I wanted to redeem myself from yesterday, I had to blow them all away. Of course, I wasn't going to tell Kira my strategy.

I kept shuffling my cards. I'd read my script enough to have some general knowledge of the story line of Peter Pan. In a nutshell, Peter and Tinker Bell sneak into the Darling family's nursery where they meet Wendy, John, and Michael. Peter and Tink teach them to fly and bring them to the island of Neverland where they have a few skirmishes with Captain Hook. Wendy's brothers join the lost boys and visit Tiger Lily, while Peter and Wendy run off to see the mystical mermaid lagoon. It ends with a final battle, Peter and his friends versus the pirates. Peter wins, and the Darlings leave Neverland and return home. The end.

At long last, Kira stopped staring at me and returned to her bunk. I heard a sigh and then the rustling of her settling into bed. I got back to studying my cards. Quietly.

The next day, I sauntered into rehearsal with greater confidence than the day before. Even Kira noticed my mood's sudden improvement.

"You seem a lot happier today than you were yesterday," Kira remarked as we lined up in the wings of the stage.

I grinned, settled into my self-made promise that I would *really* perform as Wendy and perform well.

If you can't beat 'em, join 'em. Sulking and wanting my role changed would get me nowhere, so why not try to be a little excited? It was funny how, in a matter of days, I went from dreading drama club to wishing for practice to begin. The contrast in my feelings was striking for not only Kira but also for myself. My palms were sweating but not in fear—in anticipation. It was only the second rehearsal, but something about doing this mock performance run-through sent electricity through my veins. It felt magical.

Kira looked like she was about to ask me something when we were interrupted.

Mrs. Kerrington clapped twice. "Everyone, please open your scripts to the first page. We'll be reading through the whole thing. I'll call for actors to join us onto the stage as they appear in the performance."

The area behind the stage was dark enough to make clear sight difficult, but it was easy to hear the buzzing and sense the overflowing emotions. Around me, paper crinkled as everyone prepared their packet while I stood timidly without mine.

Mrs. Kerrington strode up to me. "Where are your lines? Did you forget them at home?"

"Oh, I won't be needing the script," I said dismissively, trying to keep my cool, although I was terrified of getting in trouble.

"What do you mean? How will you read your lines?" The drama teacher furrowed her brows.

I put it simply. "I know my lines."

"Since when!"

"Since last night."

Mrs. Kerrington's mouth dropped open. "You memorized the *entire script* in one night?"

I nodded, exhilarated. This was my moment! Kids around me were astonished. Some even clapped a little. The look on Yumiko's face was priceless; she looked dumbfounded for once. I heard Kira hiss from across the room, "So *that's* what you were doing with those note cards all last night!"

Mrs. Kerrington shook her head in awe, and her lips widened slowly into a smile. "You have an excellent memory, Katelyn Dorsey. Pristine."

CHAPTER 15

Kira

"No fair," Yumiko whisper-screeched. "She's lying. She hasn't memorized the script."

I knew Katelyn had a good memory. Scratch that, it was more than good, it was extraordinary. But to memorize EVERYTHING in a matter of hours? No way. Then again, she did learn every country's capital in precisely forty-eight minutes on the car ride to the GeoBee state finals and taught herself the Pythagorean theorem—at age seven.

"Katelyn!" I shoved my way through the crowd, careful not to bump into any of the props. We were behind the stage after all, and it was dark enough to make navigation difficult.

I grabbed my sister by her shoulders and looked her dead in the eye. "You *actually* know all your lines?"

"Yes, why else would I have told Mrs. Kerrington?" Her tone was teasing, but she seemed pretty pleased with herself. I could almost say she enjoyed the attention.

"Here's the little show-off," Yumiko joined in, uninvited. "Who do you think you are?"

"Who do *you* think you are?" I retorted, sticking my nose in the air. "Seems like you're a little jealous of our lead girl."

Yumiko turned as red as the tips of her hair. "Katelyn didn't memorize those lines. That's impossible." She leaned in a little closer to my sister and lowered her voice. "Everybody knows what a fox-faced liar you are."

Katelyn's eyes narrowed deviously. "Oh yeah? Let's test that right now."

Things were going south fast, but luckily, Mrs. Kerrington came between us and dragged Katelyn and the leads out on stage. The other actors, including me, had to remain silent in the wings. Nerves were running too high to just sit there, though, so we peeked our heads through the curtains to watch as the run-through began. Seven on the stage: Jacob as Peter, Vera as Tinker Bell, Jean as Nana the dog, and three other boys as Wendy's younger brothers. They all clutched their scripts, their only lifeline. Then there my sister stood without one.

I thought back to the grouchy, introverted Katelyn that I'd known before the auditions. Never a chuckle, never a laugh. Always focused on studies. It felt so long ago. Could it really have been so recent that she'd changed? She seemed to be embracing her role and finally opening up a little. If she were a flower, she'd be blooming right about now.

Mrs. Kerrington called others up as their characters were introduced. I came up briefly during a scene with Captain Hook, but mostly I remained backstage with the many who weren't good enough to star. Mrs. Kerrington hardly had to interrupt to fix placements or to pronounce a word or to help flustered actors blunder through their monologues. Everyone performed splendidly.

And to her everlasting credit, scriptless Katelyn did not forget one single word in the entire play. Mrs. Kerrington looked astounded. Yumiko's mouth could have caught a few flies, hanging open the way it was.

After the rehearsal, Mrs. Kerrington ran up to Katelyn and me. "Girls! That was lovely!" she gushed. "And, Katelyn, I have never before seen such a supreme memory."

"Oh, it's nothing, really," Katelyn stammered, blushing. "It took hours. Anyone could do it if they tried."

The drama director patted her shoulder fondly, and I had never felt prouder of my twin. "You're going to make a wonderful Wendy!"

And then she was skipping over to the other side of the room, talking a mile a minute to a stormy-faced Yumiko.

I shook my head out of amusement and smiled. "That Mrs. Kerrington. Always in her own world."

"She sure is." Vera materialized behind us, her blond hair bobbing on her shoulders. "This play has given her so much energy. It's because we're the best she's ever cast."

Katelyn grinned. "You think?"

"For sure," Vera said. "You were great up there. Not a single stumble over your lines. And, Kira, you make a magnificent pirate."

I laughed. "You were awesome too, Vera."

She shrugged off the compliment, not out of pure modesty but in just straight-up disagreement. "I was average. Not like Katelyn."

We started to make our way out of the auditorium as the rehearsal was over. Fancy Vera and Katelyn, two former nerds, thrust into the spotlight! Vera struck me as a rather plain but outright and sensible girl, not reserved like many other honors students. Right then, I realized what she was sacrificing to take place in this performance.

"Don't you want to compete in the trivia tournament?" I blurted out then smacked a hand over my mouth. Katelyn's face fell, and at once, the carefree girl I'd met briefly disappeared. It must've been a while since she'd thought about the tournament, and now I'd stolen that blissful ignorance. A look of anguish and unsureness crossed her face.

Vera didn't notice the drop in the mood. "To be honest, I'm more interested in showbiz than all those educational contests I used to do. What about you, Katelyn?"

"I want to do it," Katelyn said shakily. "Of course, I want to do it."

"Aww, I know it sucks that you can't do both as they're scheduled for the same day," Vera said, offering sympathy. "Don't worry, there will be plenty of other tournaments in the future!"

I swallowed the bitter taste in my mouth. "She knows that."

Katelyn glared at her shoelaces. Vera looked confused and overwhelmed. I didn't blame her; she had no idea of the very intricate conflict that was at hand.

After a long pause, Vera said, "I'd better leave you guys to it."

The walk home was silent and unbearable without Vera as a mediator. Katelyn shoved her fingers deep into her pockets. I tightened my cardigan. Here we were again, just like the morning of the auditions! A house divided, twin against twin, on a brisk autumn day with too many decisions to make. If only I didn't have such a big mouth, I wouldn't have reminded Katelyn of the painful choice that stood in front of her. She was so passionate about that academic stuff, so dedicated to school. And I couldn't forget that other brainy girl she sometimes brought up in conversation, what was her name? Ella? Elena? Eleanore! I vaguely recall Katelyn complaining that Eleanore would attend the tournament and surely win without my twin as competition. Katelyn would hate having that rubbed in her face as much as I would hate to see Yumiko succeed.

I racked my brain, trying to think of a compromise. Katelyn loved the trivia tournament. Katelyn loved the play. What to do?

I've got it! In a burst of excited energy, I whirled around to my sister and beamed with delight. "We can switch places!"

Chapter 16

I was having fun with the musical. Really, I was! But the possibility of Eleanore winning the trivia tournament was enough to send me into panic mode. It had been so peaceful, the short period of time in which I had forgotten about my dilemma stress-free. But Kira had reminded me of the tournament. I didn't blame her. I was going to have to face the truth at some point that I wouldn't be able to do the tournament, period.

People have constantly mixed us twins up, especially when we were younger, and our parents dressed us in matching outfits. I'm used to being called Kira every now and then when someone forgets who is who. It happens to everyone, but we've never purposely switched places. I've read books and seen movies about twins taking on the other's identity, and to be honest, I thought it was cool, but it's never something I'd have wanted to try. There's too much risk and little reward other than a burst of confidence to do it again. Besides, I'd have no real purpose for it, and it would probably only get me in trouble. But here I am, grasping at straws, and could it be the only option?

Kira was known for conjuring up drastic measures and exotic ideas. But now she was standing before me, her brown eyes twinkling with mischief, and I couldn't comprehend the words that had just come out of her mouth, "*We can switch places!*" It echoed like a shout into the Grand Canyon. *Switch places! Switch places! Switch places!*

"No," I said in an emotionless voice. "No, we can't."

Kira jumped up and down, spilling over with ecstasy like a glass of sparkling water. "Yes, we can! Listen, what time is the tournament?"

"It's from six o'clock in the evening to seven. What are you getting at?" I answered tiredly. I could already tell the direction the conversation was going.

Kira burst into a smile. "Don't you see? The play starts at six thirty, and the second act starts at seven fifteen! There'll be a gap large enough between the two for you to take part in both and for me to have a shot at being Wendy!"

I chewed my lip worriedly. "What's your point?"

"Katy, you can do the trivia tournament! I'll pretend to be you and go on stage as Wendy for the first act while you compete in the tournament. Then you can take over as Wendy for the second act. It works perfectly since *my* character as a pirate only shows up in that final act! The second act battle, I mean, with Captain Hook against Peter Pan," Kira finished with a flourish.

What! No! This was ridiculous. I searched my twin's face for a sign of intelligence but only found childish giddiness. "I…Kira, we can't do this, it's lying!"

"Yes, we can!" she insisted, pointedly ignoring the second half of my sentence. "It's possible, and not only possible but also *practical* and *doable*. Look, I can use big words! I'm smart! And this idea is smart!"

"But then there will be two Katelyns and no Kiras, and then a Kira pretending to be a Katelyn, and then, ugh, it will never work! You've got your head in the clouds."

"My head is actually very firmly atop my shoulders. Can't you just trust me!" Kira said, exasperated. "I know what I'm doing, I swear! I've got a plan all worked out. If you could just—"

"Kira!" I sputtered. "This isn't one of your dramatic teen television shows, okay? Do you realize the amount of trouble we could get in when we get caught?"

"*If* we get caught."

I clawed at my face with my hands before letting out an anguished sigh. "Fine. Fine, Kira, I'll listen to your foolish plan, and then *maybe* we can go through with it. But it all depends on how you've got this worked out because one wrong move and—"

"And everyone will get mad at us. I know, I know, I know." But I'd agreed to listen to her, so as we walked, Kira detailed to me every twist and turn of her extravagant plan. We would walk to Pine Hills Academy and sign in at the auditorium. With both Kira and Katelyn's names on the attendance sheet, hopefully, everyone would think we were both there, except we wouldn't be. Because at the first opportunity I got, I would sneak out of the auditorium and head to the other side of the school: the gymnasium. There, the trivia tournament would begin at six, and with any luck, nobody would notice that I'd be signed into both the tournament and the play because that would surely raise eyebrows. I would compete in the tournament just like normal, whilst Kira would manipulate Mrs. Kerrington into thinking that both of us were in the auditorium when it was really only one. At six thirty precisely, the play would begin, and Kira would run through the first act as me, in my role, as Wendy. At seven, the tournament would end, and I'd sneak back into the auditorium where I would meet Kira backstage. She'd hand over the Wendy costume, and—fingers crossed—I'd be ready for the second act at seven fifteen. She would get into her pirate costume, and we'd be good to go. At the end of the second act, we'd take a bow, greet our family as they gushed over how wonderful we were, and go home as if no tricks had been played. The issue was, there were way too many *if*s and *hopefully*s and *with luck*s. The risk was real, and the odds were most certainly against everything going right.

The plan was just as bonkers as I expected it to be. "Too many loopholes, Kira. I mean, do you really think nobody would notice me signing into both events? Really?" Kira groaned, but I kept talking. "And all of this depends so heavily on timing. What if the trivia tournament ran late? Or what if the second act started early?" I threw my hands up in frustration. "This is nuts!"

"It's not!" Kira's body language told me everything I needed to know: the chewing of the lip, the tense shoulders, and the quick but certain stride. Kira was not going to back down. I knew I had better talk some sense into her or else I'd fall down the rabbit hole of ridicule just like she had.

"Surely someone will find out about our trading-places business, even if it's not right away. Someone—Eleanore's mom, I don't know—will mention to Mom about me in the tournament and then we'll be in for it."

Kira kicked a pebble into the street. "That's not important. We can't dwell on the things that could go wrong, we have to trust the things that can go right."

Huh?

"Your reputation," Kira continued, "is what you want to maintain. Right? This is about beating Eleanore and being known as the smartest sixth grader at Pine Hills. Just like being in the play, for me, is about showing Yumiko that I'm worth more than hair ribbons and ponytails."

"It's not *just* about Eleanore," I said softly, even though it was blatantly obvious that most of it were. I faltered here, not knowing what else I should say.

Kira filled in the blanks. "You just want to be noticed. It's okay, I get it, I want attention too. And this plan is going to solve all our problems, so let's quit the drama and get a move on!"

We walked in silence for the next few blocks, lost in our own thoughts. This whole situation was getting blown up into WAY more than it needed to be. You would've thought our lives depending on the contest and the play, but when you're twelve years old, what else is of importance?

We'd just turned into the driveway when Kira whispered, "Katelyn, trust me just this once. I promise I won't let you down."

It took a whole lot of convincing for the rest of the evening, but finally, I agreed.

73

CHAPTER 17

Kira

I had everything laid out perfectly in my head. I just needed my sister to cooperate with the plan, which, for the moment, she was, but you never know how fast someone can change their mind. Luckily, having Katelyn on my team would surely open up a more logical and analytical side of my "extravagant" scheme.

The next few days spiraled past like a whirlwind. Katelyn and I made a deal not to tell anyone about what we were doing, not even our parents. Sharing our plan would just end up with us in a world of trouble. On the other hand, I had to privately rehearse not only my role as a pirate but also as Wendy. If I were to be a lead for the first act, I'd better know my lines and, oh boy, there were *so many* lines! If I hadn't been mind-boggled before, I was even more astonished by the speed at which Katelyn had memorized all these. Yeah, she was a genius, but what kind of genius can memorize a two-act, fifty-page, hour-and-a-half musical in just one night? Each evening before we went to bed, Katy worked with me to learn my lines by pushing and prompting me. Even then, it was a tiring struggle.

One night, I let the script fall loosely at my feet for the tenth time as I let out a sigh of frustration. "It's no use! I'll never be able to memorize all this. We may as well give up on the plan."

Katelyn shook her head indignantly, her brown curls bouncing at her cheeks. "You forced me to agree to this, and we're going through with it."

I pouted and kicked the script around a little with my toes, trying to appear as feeble as possible. Maybe if she thought I was pitiful enough, Katelyn would let me off the hook, but Katelyn never lets anyone off the hook.

"Pick up your script," Katelyn said patiently. "Let's go through this again. Start at the beginning."

I did as she said. My sister must have inherited all the chill genes because, at the moment, I was fed up while she was keeping her head. I was trying so hard to remember my lines, especially after I'd fought so hard for Katelyn to agree to this. I wasn't going to let it all go down the drain now.

It took about another half an hour before we gave up for the night. I'd only barely memorized about the first three pages, which was less than admirable. Additionally, I had my lines as a pirate to memorize, which was only a few ARRRS and AHOYS here and there, but still another task to be completed.

School was not only a bore but also now a distraction. I was rehearsing for the musical while simultaneously being smothered by the boatload of homework my teachers assigned me. My daily schedule consisted of school, rehearsal with Mrs. Kerrington, then those secret rehearsals at home with my sister, and finally studying. I was lucky if I ended up with half an hour before bed to relax.

Abby caught wind of my exhaustion one day as we were traveling between classes. She came up behind me and elbowed me teasingly. "Why are you so down in the dumps, Kira? Normally you're bursting with energy!"

I shrugged as we passed groups of chattering classmates along the hallway. Everyone else was exchanging books or gossiping or double-checking their locker, and what was I doing? Moping about. "I don't know, I've just been feeling tired lately."

"Oh, I bet you are!" Abby laughed. "With these rehearsals and all. I've been bending over backward designing the set! We're all feeling a little worn out."

When I didn't respond, she stepped in front of me and swiveled around, pinning me against someone's locker. "Come on, Kira. I know you better than this. What's up?"

I glanced around nervously before lowering my voice. "Can you keep a secret?"

Abby rolled her eyes and elbowed me again. "You know I can."

The plan had been itching me all day; I just had to tell someone about it. Katelyn wasn't much of a pleasure to talk to, and I was dying to explain to someone how I was feeling. Still, with the risk of all these other kids roaming around, I dragged her into the girls' bathroom across the hall where we could have some privacy. Leaning against the sink, I took a deep breath and tried to explain the source of my angst.

"The workload is a lot," I said, "especially with homework and rehearsals and—" I paused and scraped the tiled floor with the toe of my sneakers. My heart was beginning to pound.

"Go on," encouraged Abby, her tone gentle. "Whatever it is, you can tell me. I won't be mad."

I knew Katelyn would murder me for what I was about to do, but it didn't matter. I had to get this off my chest, and Abby was a good secret keeper. Katelyn would never find out about it anyway.

"Katelyn and I are switching places," I blurted out. I crossed my fingers behind my back, praying that I hadn't just made a huge mistake.

The initial look of confusion registered on Abby's face before developing into amusement. "Is that it?" She laughed, her eyes twinkling.

I furrowed my brow. This wasn't the reaction I was expecting. "I mean, well, no, but I—"

"Don't all twins switch places at some time or another?" Abby said bluntly. She furrowed her brow and tilted her chin just so, in that special way, that only she can do. That way in which she could get anyone to spill all their secrets.

I just stared at her. This was not the reaction I had been expecting. I was preparing for an *"Oh no, you can't do that! You'll get in trouble!"*

"I mean, I've never had a twin, so I wouldn't really know," she added hastily after seeing the dumbfounded look on my face.

I waved my hands quickly as if wiping away a wrong notion. "No, no, that's not what I meant. I thought you'd be mad or something, because—"

Maybe I should've shut my mouth there and then, especially after the deal Katelyn and I made about not telling anyone, ever, but I told Abby everything: about Katelyn's tough decision between the play and the trivia tournament, about the plan I hatched and how she agreed to it, and about how I would secretly be playing Wendy in the first act. I babbled endlessly about our big twin-switch idea whilst staring guiltily down at my shoes and wondering at what degree of anger Katelyn would react to me spilling the beans. She was already so terrified of the prospect of trouble that I'm sure she wouldn't be at all pleased with me. Luckily, Abby just nodded understandingly and looked thoughtful. She didn't once interrupt me or advise me not to go through with the plan.

When I was finished, there was a brief pause before Abby spoke up. "Wow. That's…creative. It sounds just like the kind of thing you see in movies. Would you like me to keep it a secret?"

"Yes, oh yes, please," I gushed, forever grateful that I had such a good friend. Maybe Katelyn wouldn't have to hear about this after all.

We'd just scooped up our backpacks, prepared to leave, and hoped that we wouldn't get in too much trouble for being late to our next class when the worst thing possible happened.

The sound of a toilet flushing emanated from the inside of the last stall, and that could only mean one thing.

Somebody had just listened to every word I'd said.

I froze in terror. Abby's eyes widened, and I scrambled to swallow the bitter taste that was emerging from the back of my throat. My eyes bounced back and forth between Abby's petrified expression and the stall like a miniature game of ping-pong.

"Hello?" I said tentatively. The stall door flung open.

Out stepped none other than Eleanore Anderson, her lace-up cowgirl boots polished and pretty.

CHAPTER 18

Katelyn

Science, physical education, history—those were my upcoming classes, so I tossed my math textbook listlessly into my locker and dragged out my biology and social studies ones. I debated grabbing an extra binder too for good measure. You can never be too prepared. But since my arms were already overflowing with materials, I decided I'd be okay without one.

As I gathered my supplies, I recited trivia facts to myself in preparation for the competition. Last night, I'd made myself some flashcards, color-coded by subject and difficulty, to practice. I was working as hard as I could to stuff as much knowledge into my brain as possible; however, it was still a challenging and demanding task. To make matters worse, I had to practice in secret at night due to the fact that nobody could know I was participating in both *Peter Pan* and the trivia tournament. Well, I was going to grit my teeth and push through it, and with any luck, I'd be prepared and ready to win.

"Which month's name is derived from the Latin word for eight?" I tested myself. "Easy. October, duh."

"How many medals did gymnast Mary Lou Retton win in the 1984 Summer Olympics? Five."

"The twenty-fifth president of the United States was sworn in on January 29, 1843. What was his name? William McKinley."

It went on like this, a rapid-fire quiz of my own smarts as I unpacked and repacked my backpack with supplies. Once I had set the last pencil into its compartment, I scooped up my pack and swung it over my shoulder. I was just preparing to dart off to class when I felt a tap on my shoulder and heard a tinkly voice holler my name.

"Hey, Katelyn!"

I almost jumped out of my skin. Had I been reciting my facts too loud? I'd made a pointed effort to keep my voice low so nobody could hear what I was saying. They'd certainly suspect I was practicing for the tournament. Once they put two and two together about me also being Wendy in the musical, the game would be up. I whirled around, bracing myself for the worst.

Instead, I found myself face-to-face with a freckled button nose and two glittering blue eyes. I sighed with relief. It was only Vera Smith, my co-star in *Peter Pan*. My secret was still safe.

Vera plopped her hands on her hips, oblivious to the mess that would've just occurred if she questioned my trivia-reciting intentions. "Hey, Katelyn!" she repeated. "Do you have plans for tonight?"

"N-no," I stammered, startled by the unexpected question. "Well, you and I both have drama rehearsal, of course, and then I have to help Kira learn, I mean, help Kira with her homework. What about you?"

Vera shrugged. "I don't have much going on after rehearsal. I have some studying to do, of course, but that'll be easy."

"Oh," I said plainly. I probably should've said something a bit more gratifying, but I was still learning the ropes of this social stuff. And didn't I have a class to get to? I felt exposed and awkward, clutching my books against my chest and leaning against a locker while harried students zoomed through the hall. Normally, I'd get to my class straight after I'd exchanged my textbooks, so why was I chatting and making myself late?

"Anyway," said Vera, "since we're friends, I was wondering if you'd like to join me during study hall? We can work together!"

My jaw dropped. I shouldn't have been so shocked, but in all my twelve years of life, I'd never really had someone, besides Kira, ask me to hang out with them. I'd always been known as the quiet, bookish kid, and nobody was ever interested in talking to me. I guess I gave off the wrong vibes; maybe I should've made an effort to appear at least *approachable*. A social life was never for me, but Mr. Clark was right, this whole *Peter Pan* thing was really helping me become more friendly and comfortable around others. And now Vera, the girl I used to be only vaguely acquainted with from my honors classes, had called me her friend!

"Of course," I sputtered. "Let's go before we're tardy. Whoever's monitoring study hall wouldn't be very impressed with us turning up late."

Vera nodded. "You're right. You know, I've never seen you do this before."

We started on our way to room 102 where study hall would take place. I tried to keep cool, wondering feverishly how I should act. But Vera's statement unnerved me: "*I've never seen you do this before.*" What hadn't I been doing?

Vera seemed to read my thoughts. "Hang out with friends, I mean. You're always either alone or with Kira."

I felt my face grow hot. I knew I was a loner, but did I really look like it? Was I so withdrawn? I thought of all the times I'd coldly brushed off many of the girls in my class whenever they said hello. All those times when I spent lunch in a corner reading a book in solitary unless Kira decided to come over and talk to me. I was so dependent on my sister for socialization, and I hadn't even noticed.

I took a shaky breath, unsure of how to respond. "I guess so. I always...I always thought—" I trailed off, trying desperately to quicken my pace as I walked. If only room 102 wasn't so far down the hall; I wished this conversation could end.

"Go on," Vera encouraged.

"I always thought friends were a waste of time," I blurted out. "There, I said it."

"A waste of time?" Vera was baffled. She glanced at me sideways, her blue eyes searching my face for answers.

"Until I met you," I added, flustered. "I thought friends were a distraction from my studies."

Vera looked thoughtful. She was silent as we entered the study hall and took adjacent seats at a table. She didn't speak until a solid minute had passed, and I was examining my own fingernails. She said, "Your academics aren't everything, Katelyn."

I looked up, agitated. The room monitor's eyes darted swiftly around the room. Study hall was a no-talking zone, and Vera was breaking the rules. I didn't feel like dealing with another detention, so I kept my voice lowered to a husky whisper. "I know. Kira tells me that every day."

"Maybe you should start listening to Kira," Vera suggested, and I had a feeling that she was only half joking. Out of my peripheral vision, I noticed the room monitor's head jerk over to our direction, sniffing the air as if she could smell out our words like a dog. I yanked out a random textbook so I could look busy and hopefully fool the monitor. Vera took the message and did the same, and the monitor turned away.

Keeping my eyes firmly glued to the page of my science book, I murmured, "Probably. But half the things that come out of her mouth make me feel like her brain is full of cotton candy and lemon drops."

Vera swallowed a laugh, and even though she was gazing down at her textbook, I could see her eyes twinkling. "And yours is full of flashcards and IQ tests. Intelligence can only get a girl so far, and that's coming from an honors kid!"

I kept forgetting that Vera was in all the advanced classes because she was *nothing like me*. She wasn't a nerd or a geek, she was an ordinary kid who kept a healthy balance between school and friends. I was learning how to do that right now.

We spent the rest of the class period whispering to each other about this and that, averting the room monitor's sharklike gaze, and really doing no actual studying at all. I thought about how it was so fun to have someone to talk to besides Kira, someone who I could joke with and who could understand me. I found myself disappointed when the bell rang, signaling the end of the class. I half-heartedly scooped my books into my backpack and prepared for my next subject.

I was just turning around to leave when I heard Vera's hesitant "wait."

I could tell by her tone that something wasn't right. I turned on a dime and held my breath. "What's up?"

"I know this sounds like a weird question, but I'm just curious. What were you whispering about back at the lockers? Before I said 'hey'?" The innocent look on her face showed that she was merely curious. I'm sure she didn't mean to be nosy. "I don't want to sound rude or anything, I was just wondering since we don't have any tests today.

"No, you aren't rude. I was just...practicing something...for schoolwork," I strained, barely able to string my words together. This was exactly what I was praying *wouldn't* happen. I made a mental note to be more careful next time because getting caught out would land me in a world of trouble. I could only hope that Kira had the sense to keep her word and do the same.

Vera cocked her head to the side and my heart quickly filled with dread. "Are you sure?"

"Yes, I'm sure."

Vera looked doubtful, but after contemplating it for a second, she just nodded and accepted my response as truth. "Okay. See you later!"

I gulped and waved her goodbye. I had better get to class.

CHAPTER 19

Kira

Eleanore Anderson!

Of all the people in the world. Of course, it had to be Katelyn's greatest enemy. I gritted my teeth and tried to swallow my fear, glaring into the dark and unforgiving eyes of Eleanore.

For a moment, the three of us just stood there, speechless. Eleanore with her hands set firmly on her hips, her lips curled into a smirk. Abby with her palm covering her mouth so no noise would be allowed to escape. And me, making a desperate attempt at concealing my horror. How on earth was I going to recover from this? Eleanore knew our secret! It was over. I was dead meat.

"Well," Eleanore hissed, breaking the tense silence. "I'd better not just have heard what I think I heard. Because if I did, the Dorsey twins are breaking the school rules and are, therefore, punishable with an expulsion."

Was I supposed to respond to that? Was I supposed to say yes? Yes, indeed, the Dorsey twins were breaking rules to an extreme degree. Yes, if we were caught out, there was a 99 percent chance we would get expelled and probably grounded too for all eternity. This was not part of the plan. I should've kept my stupid fat mouth shut and stuck to the deal Katelyn and I made! Why did I break that promise?

I wobbled dangerously, my feet threatening to tip me over. "You don't know that."

Eleanore guffawed. "Nice try, but I'm pretty sure lying to your drama teacher, pretending to be each other, and sneaking in and out of various rooms is not something the principal would encourage." Her dark eyes flickered wickedly. She took a breath before continuing. "Besides, don't you value honesty? I'm sure Katelyn would hate to get into a colossal amount of trouble, especially after maintaining a flawless record all these years."

I stood there in silence, unable to respond. Abby took a step forward, closing the three-yard gap between us and the villain.

"Don't," I whispered to her. "You'll only make it worse."

"I know what I'm doing," she murmured out of the corner of her mouth. She kept her eyes firmly locked on Eleanore's.

"So you think Kira and Katelyn are the rulebreakers?" Abby said sharply, using a tone of voice I'd never heard from her before. "I don't think anyone's forgotten you and your mom's trick at the spelling bee last year. Mouthing answers to you? Pathetic."

Eleanore's face paled to nearly white before cycling through about seven violent shades of red. I bet Abby could use those crimsons for painting *Peter Pan*'s set. And I couldn't help wondering how incredibly late for class we must be.

Abby ventured closer, raising her voice. "And the fourth-grade science fair? Funny how you and Katelyn's projects were exactly the same."

Several choked noises escaped Eleanore's mouth before she shook her head firmly. Blinking a few times, she said viciously, "Stupid Katelyn copied me. Everyone knows that."

"Then explain why *I* saw Katelyn complete hers first? Before you," Abby retorted. "It's obvious that you only turned your project in first so *she'd* look like a copycat."

My eyes darted between the two girls, fearing that the argument was going a bit too far. "Guys, I think—"

I couldn't force the words out. Eleanore glowered mercilessly at Abby. "You're not an honors student. You know less than you think you do, Abigail."

They stood facing each other at about a yard's distance like two Wild West outlaws preparing for a showdown. It was an ominous ten seconds that we stood there in silence before Eleanore took the bait.

"Let's make a deal," Eleanore said hushedly, squinting at Abby like an eagle sighting its prey. "You keep your mouth shut about… about the things I did, and I won't tell *anyone* that the Dorseys are switching places."

A deal. This could either prove to be a genius idea or go terribly, horribly wrong. Assuming that both Abigail and Eleanore followed up on this pact, nobody would hear about Eleanore cheating or me swapping places with Katy, but there were too many variables. For example, what if Katelyn won the trivia tournament? Would Eleanore use her newfound knowledge to get my sister eliminated and steal the crown? Possibly. But if Abby upheld her side of the deal, that would mean Eleanore would land herself in trouble too. It was a stalemate, a deadlock, an impasse. I had gotten myself into yet another dilemma.

I realized that Eleanore was looking expectantly at Abby, studying her face, trying to deduce whether she would accept or decline the deal.

Abby's hands curled into fists beside her. Her cheeks puffed in and out, and I could tell that she was analyzing every consequence of accepting Eleanore's offer and calculating the downsides of refusing it. I'd never seen her quite so fired up.

"Deal," Abby said at last. "We won't say a word, assuming that you don't either."

Eleanore nodded stiffly, bitter yet satisfied. Thank goodness this had all cooled down. I let out the breath I hadn't realized I was holding, but Eleanore wasn't finished. "And you, Kira?"

I gulped, straightening my spine and aiming to look as fearless as possible. It wasn't working. "Yeah?"

"One false move, and everybody hears about your *plan*." With that, she stormed past us both with a thundering glare on her face and slammed the bathroom door shut on the way out.

*****

Abby and I kept a low profile for the rest of the day. Fortunately, Eleanore was in all the advanced classes, so we didn't run into her again. Even so, I was paranoid that Katelyn and I were doomed after the confrontation. Things were not looking good.

When the bell rang at three thirty, I sighed with relief. Drama rehearsal was next, my favorite part of the day! My heart skipped a beat when I remembered today was our first rehearsal in which we would sing. With my official role being what it was, *I* wouldn't be doing much singing, but my sister would. I'd seen Katelyn sing once at the auditions, in which she did quite well, considering the circumstances. She definitely had potential, but would she be able to handle singing through an entire musical at a real rehearsal? I guess I'd just have to find out.

I passed Katelyn on my way to the auditorium. I almost disregarded her, but then I realized with a start she was talking and laughing with another kid. It was Vera Smith, the pixie-like girl who'd landed the part of Tinker Bell. Out of curiosity, I pursued the pair, leaving a far-enough distance that I would remain unnoticed. For once, Katelyn seemed to have found a friend.

Wendy and Tinker Bell—enemies in the storyline, best friends in real life? Vera, with her silky blond hair that barely scraped below her chin and her wide blue eyes and button nose—absolutely perfect material for the role of Tinker Bell. Mrs. Kerrington was no fool with her casting.

I followed them into the auditorium where the rehearsal was just beginning. Scripts rustled, and hushed lines flew across the room as kids prepared to step onto the stage. Mrs. Kerrington wandered around, occasionally assisting the crew as they put together the beginnings of the set. Half-painted backdrops, cardboard trees, and fairy lights were being sorted out of a tangled heap. I spotted Abby among the ruckus and waved to her. Yumiko was there also, not with the crew but instead her snotty little circle of friends, flitting around like a ladybug with an antsy expression on her face. She looked eager to recover from the embarrassment she'd experienced last rehearsal.

A crisp clap from Mrs. Kerrington dissolved the noise in the room. "All right, everyone, we're going to start by singing through all the songs. It was expected that you would have practiced them at home with your scripts. You may still use them now, but you should have these tunes memorized and be script-free by next week."

Groans and protests erupted throughout the crowd as nobody wanted to have to memorize such a large section of the play by Mrs. Kerrington's deadline. She took no notice of everyone's obvious displeasure and continued strictly along with the schedule.

"We will start with the opening chorus. This scene will require Peter, Wendy, Tinker Bell—"

CHAPTER 20

Katelyn

I tried to swallow my terror at the prospect of singing in front of a crowd again. The audition had been hard enough, and I'd only had to sing a few lines there. Now I would have to recite multiple songs. Across the room, I noticed Kira eyeing me closely, probably waiting for me to shrivel up out of fright.

I joined Vera and Jacob Thompson, the boy who'd been granted the role of Peter Pan himself, upon the stage. We were followed by the boys who were to play Wendy's brothers and Mrs. Darling—the role I had been determined to get. Jacob looked as smug as ever, cool, and confident in the spotlight. If Vera was nervous, she didn't show it at all. I felt insignificant next to both of them, praying that my panic was not being displayed on my face.

Right then, it hit me that I was standing in front of everyone—Kira, Mrs. Kerrington, everyone—preparing to rehearse. The lights were dim, and I had dozens of strangers staring at me, judging me, and waiting for me to perform. I blinked fast and reminded myself that this was not the first time I would have to do this; that I would eventually have to do this in front of parents too.

I looked down at the script in my trembling hands. I wouldn't be needing it to remember the song, but since I'd already made my statement last rehearsal, I resolved that it was time to blend among the others again. No more showing off. I raised it to where I could see it, and my costars did the same. My eyes made one last desperate round of the audience, and the piano started to play the first notes of the opening song.

Jacob sang the first line, his voice clear as day. He was accompanied by Vera for the second and third lines. Neither of them appeared to have any reservations about performing in front of an audience, an ability I'd always failed to develop. Next to this pair, I was going to look and sound like a donkey.

My thoughts had overwhelmed me, and all of a sudden, it was my turn, my line. The pounding of my head drowned out the piano, and I was sure I was bound to faint again. Dark spots danced before my eyes, and taking steady breaths became a challenge. I tried to force myself to sing, but no sound came out. Someone jabbed me in the ribs, probably Jacob, prompting me to begin. The pain, dull as it was, jarred me back to reality. Mortified, my head snapped up, and I started to sing.

Thank goodness I wasn't embarrassingly bad at singing. If I hadn't been able to carry a tune, we'd have other problems to worry about, but I succeeded in keeping my voice stable and on key. All the same, I was glad when it was over. I had victoriously managed to pull myself together and stumble through the song without too many mishaps. Still, I could tell by the strained smile on Mrs. Kerrington's face that she was having second thoughts on the casting of Wendy.

I followed Vera, Jacob, and the rest of the group off the stage, keeping my head low and trying to avoid the scrutinizing looks that were being thrown in my direction. At least I could take a break to recover while several other small groups performed. I took my place in the audience alongside my sister, who immediately slung her arm over my shoulder. My face crumpled.

"Hey, don't freak out," Kira said softly. "It really wasn't bad. Your singing was fine. You'll do better next time."

I blinked fast. "I have more songs to do! How will I be able to get through them?"

Kira gestured toward the crowd. "All these kids, everyone is nervous. You're not alone. You're going to sing."

I tried to breathe normally, but I felt like hyperventilating. "Okay. Okay." Then I looked back at all the kids who'd be watching me, and I crumpled into my seat. "I can't do it."

Kira stared at me, and for a moment I was afraid she was going to smack me. Then she yanked my arm and dragged me toward the auditorium exit doors.

I struggled against her grip, flailing around frantically. "Kira! What are you doing? Where are we—"

My sister slapped her palm over my mouth and gritted her teeth. "Be quiet, or else people will notice we're gone."

The auditorium doors slammed shut behind us. I gazed longingly behind me at the students rehearsing inside, but Kira continued to incessantly haul me down the corridor. She stopped once we'd reached the girls' bathrooms, stuck her head inside and looked around wildly, and then threw me in like a rag doll.

"Ow," I said, landing awkwardly on my shoulder. Kira shut the hefty bathroom door and wedged the doorstop into place. Then she pivoted around, facing me, a smug grin painted across her face.

"If we're going to switch places for the show, we'd better start practicing," Kira proclaimed with a flourish.

I rubbed my shoulder, miffed. "So you're saying we should switch places for the rehearsals? That sounds pretty reckless to me."

Kira slouched against the door and rolled her eyes. "Not all the rehearsals, silly. That *would* be reckless. Just this one, to start. I'll sing your songs and act your parts, and all will be well."

She paused. I could tell she was beginning to realize how stupid she sounded. I wondered for the thousandth time why I'd agreed to go through with her little plan.

She shook her head as if to clear it. "Just this once. A practice round. To test if we really look alike enough to pull this off." Kira smirked a little. "Besides, I'll be getting you out of singing."

That settled it for me. I exhaled the breath I forgot I'd been holding and said, "Deal."

From there on, it was a flurry of turmoil and adrenaline as we swapped clothing, hairstyles, and shoes. I fiddled with buckles and zippers, wondering frenziedly how my sister put this stuff on each morning. I felt tangled in a too-bright assortment of Kira's wardrobe and almost blinded myself with the monstrosity that was her outfit choice.

At long last, I had buttoned the final button, and we stepped aside after finishing our tangent of exchanging clothes. I stared at myself in the bathroom mirror. I was wearing Kira's pink T-shirt, sky-blue denim skirt, and white checkered Vans. My hair was tied up with an excessively glittery band, one strand let loose beside my face. Kira's hair was down around her shoulders, and she was wearing my drab sweatpants and chartreuse sweater. My worn-out sneakers looked two sizes too small on her feet; the laces flailed around helplessly. The person standing directly before me definitely wasn't Katelyn Dorsey. The reflection beside my own wasn't Kira. We had victoriously transformed into an exact likeness of each other.

"Wow," Kira murmured. "I'm you."

"You don't make a very good Katelyn," I sniffed. "Katelyn would never wear those ridiculous earrings."

Kira's hands flew to her ears and hurriedly unclipped her earrings on both sides and slipped them into her pockets. "Couldn't have forgotten those." She laughed nervously. "Would've given us away."

I looked myself up and down. "Let's go before someone notices we're missing."

Kira straightened her shirt and lifted her chin, looking a lot more confident than I felt. "You're right. We can't mess this up."

I reminded myself that from this point forward, my name was Kira, and I was a diva.

CHAPTER 21

Kira

I felt completely out of place when I returned to the auditorium as my sister. It was like I was in the wrong body or something like my character in a video game had suddenly gotten a downgrade. We took our seats in the auditorium and observed other cast members' rehearsals while waiting for Wendy's next musical number to arrive—and arrive it did.

Mrs. Kerrington read off a few character names and invited Katelyn (me) back onto the stage for our next song. I thanked my lucky stars that my sister had forced me to learn all her lines or else I'd be in deep water with all these verses.

I could feel Katelyn's anxious eyes on my back as I took my place next to several other characters in the spotlight. I gave her a reassuring wink at least—I hoped it looked like that and not a random eye spasm—and assumed a confident posture. On second thought, I slouched back into Katelyn's miserable stoop. This was much more realistic. Katelyn would never be caught dead looking so fearless.

"All right," Mrs. Kerrington said with a tired sigh, checking her wristwatch. "Remember to consider what scene you'll be singing this piece in. Your tone must be frantic and breathless, but remember to stay in tune and make it count!"

Her eyes swept the four kids standing on the stage. I could've sworn she lingered on me the longest, and for a moment, I felt self-conscious. Did I really look enough like Katelyn? Could she tell that I wasn't her? My fingers instinctively flew to my ears, but no, my earrings were in my pocket, thanks to my sister's excellent memory.

Mrs. Kerrington tapped a few buttons on her laptop, and the background music for this scene began. I closed my eyes and let the words flow out of my mouth like honey. I was vaguely aware of Peter Pan and Smee and Captain Hook singing beside me, but everything else melted into a mountain of mushy colors and shapes. I willed myself to remember each line.

The end of the music met us faster than a bullet train, and I couldn't believe it was already over. I searched the audience wildly for my sister and found her glowing with excitement and pride. She clapped ferociously and mouthed a few words I couldn't make out, but that didn't matter because her expression alone spoke a thousand words. Apparently, I'd done something right.

Mrs. Kerrington snapped to regain our attention. "That was stupendous! Dynamite. Fabulously done. Katelyn, I'm so glad to see that you've found your place in performing!"

Kira, I thought. *Kira, not Katelyn.* "Thank you so much, I'm having so much fun!"

Mrs. Kerrington smiled curtly before moving on to notes for Peter, Hook, and Smee. Her voice dissolved into background buzz as I absorbed the victory of my first twin switch.

I looked out into the audience again. Katelyn was still gazing up at me admiringly, and I felt a surge of honor. For once, *I* was the twin to be looked up to! Yumiko didn't look at all pleased; she was staring daggers at me, clearly offended by my (Katelyn's) marvelous performance. But a few rows across from her, I noticed Vera squinting madly at me as if I was the Mona Lisa or something else to be evaluated. I couldn't understand what her deal was, but I didn't pay it too much mind; this was *my* moment!

I found myself being escorted back into my place beside Katelyn. She hugged me and whispered in my ear, "Thanks for covering for me."

I shrugged her off as if to say, "*No big deal.*" "I make a half-decent Wendy, don't I?"

"More than half decent," Katelyn said firmly. "You easily pass yourself off as me."

We settled in to observe the rest of the musical numbers, watching almost everyone do their part, however small. I sang on stage a few times more for a couple of group pieces and one short solo. Before I knew it, Mrs. Kerrington announced the end of the rehearsal.

I stood up and flexed my shoulders. I took Katelyn's hand, and we weaved between throngs of students and out of our row. We were just about to sneak away to the bathrooms to swap clothing again when Vera and Abby bounded up from behind us. Judging solely off their expressions, they both seemed vastly impressed with my (Katelyn's) performance, particularly Abby, which was interesting because she didn't really know my sister so well. I looked down at myself still dressed in my sister's clothing and then at Katelyn in mine.

"Oh my gosh, that was amazing!" Abby gushed, facing me. "You absolutely rocked the stage, Katelyn. And I thought Kira was the only performer in the family!"

Katelyn and I laughed. If only she knew it wasn't Katy singing but me!

"I can't wait to see your finished set," Katelyn (as me) said, diverting the conversation. I could tell it felt weird for both of us to be called the wrong name. Either way, Katelyn was going to have to do some acting herself if she wanted to pass off as Kira. "I bet it's worthy of the Metropolitan Museum of Art."

"I second that!" Vera chimed in.

Abby waved her hand dismissively. "Don't be ridiculous, you two. It'll suffice for a sixth-grade play."

She looked over her shoulder abruptly, and I saw Mrs. Kerrington waving her over with a folder in hand. Abby rolled her eyes. "Looks like Kerrington wants me again. Let's see who spilled a bucket of pink paint on the cardboard bushes this time around."

She skipped off to attend to our drama teacher's needs, dodging hordes of cast members as she went. Vera turned toward me, her blue eyes glinting. "You're so talented, honestly! I don't know much about music, but your singing voice was immaculate, Kira."

I was about to thank her when my heart dropped like a stone. Kira. She had just called me by my real name! I looked around frantically, and then back at Vera, my face painted with guilt. Katelyn had gone chalk white. How had we already been caught out on our very first switch?

"How did you figure it out?" I said in a low voice, my tone urgent.

Vera shook her head as if to ease my worries. "It was only your fingernails that got me. Yours, Kira's, are always flawlessly polished and trimmed, and Katelyn's have been bitten to death. Don't worry, I doubt anyone else noticed."

Katelyn visibly relaxed. "So we're in the clear?"

"In the clear," Vera confirmed. "Don't fret, you guys look exactly like each other. The nails tipped me off only because I was already suspicious, what with that weird locker whispering from this morning." She gave my sister a meaningful look like an inside joke kind of thing, but this only confused me. What had my sister done earlier in the day? Somehow, knowing she'd slipped up too comforted me. After all, I'd had my run-in with Eleanore that had almost sabotaged us, and Katelyn really didn't need to know about that little incident.

"Anyway," Vera said, "I know you have your reasons for switching places, and I've got an inkling of what those reasons are. But just know that if you're ever in a tight situation, you can count on me to help."

Kira and I shared a smile. It was good to know we had a mutual friend.

CHAPTER 22

Katelyn

The following weeks passed in a thrilling blur of rehearsals and practice. Thankfully, Kira and I didn't have to switch identities again since that last time as I gained confidence in my singing and performing. I was growing more and more comfortable in the spotlight. I felt like I had—quite literally—found my voice. Mrs. Kerrington gradually infused the musical numbers with choreography and more actual *acting*, and it really seemed like the play was coming together. Most of the cast members had nailed the memorization of their lines, the blocking, singing, and almost all of the choreography. We even managed to stumble through a few full run-throughs of the entire musical! The date of the performance drew near, and I was as ready as I could ever be.

Vera was supportive and encouraging, always there to talk about stage fright or whatever was bothering me. Her personality was the opposite of the brazen Tinker Bell's; she was sweet and charitable and everything you'd ever want in a friend. Abby was always there to help as well, not so much considering she was more Kira's bestie than mine but still polite and comradely. She'd almost completely finished the intricate set design for the play: several backdrops, painted props, and a vast assortment of lights and machines that I had no idea how to operate.

Yumiko seemed to be giving me the cold shoulder. She never once regarded me during rehearsal. As long as I didn't chicken out or injure myself, she wouldn't be performing as she was only my under-study. Of course, she would know her chance of taking my place was slim, but even so, she continued to ignore my presence. Maybe she was trying to psych me out. Thank goodness I'd gotten over most of my stage fright and tongue-tiedness on stage.

Eleanore didn't seem to be a problem. I barely spoke to her at all, which was good, because I really didn't need her to intimidate me into quitting the tournament or something. I was studying so hard: using my flashcards at any spare minute I got, researching random factoids on the Internet, and getting Vera to quiz me on what I knew. My brain felt full to bursting; I had learned so much. I could really take home the trophy in this competition. How satisfying it would be to see Eleanore cry!

At home, I drilled Kira on my lines, songs, and choreography. It didn't take long for her to get the hang of memorization, and before either of us could believe it, she'd learned the whole first act of Wendy, which she'd be playing. I wondered what had happened to the stubborn little girl with the terrible memory and what had caused the sudden improvement. Sheer adrenaline, perhaps? All I knew was that we were both prepared for our meticulously constructed twin-switch plan. I spoke to Kira the Friday night before the big show.

"So this is it," I murmured from my bottom bunk. "Can you believe it's all gone by so fast?"

Kira ruffled her covers. "I still feel like the cast list had just come out yesterday and you fainted."

I laughed softly. "And I feel like you'd only just told me that you wanted to switch places, and I was like, no way!"

Kira giggled. For five solid minutes, neither of us said anything. Then I heard my sister's timid voice drifting down to my bunk. "Katelyn, do you really think we could pull this off?"

I hesitated to answer. Logically, there was a vast number of things that could go wrong, and we could get into enormous trou-ble. But from my smart-girl standpoint? We had it all calculated out pretty well.

"Yes," I said firmly. "We've got this."

*****

My mother shook me awake the next morning. It was Saturday, and tonight, everything we'd worked on would boil down to the tournament and the play.

"Wake up, Katy! Wake up!" Mom repeated, grinning. I blinked.

Kira groaned from the top bunk. "Look, I get that today's an exciting day and all," she mumbled sleepily, "but did you really need to wake us up at six in the morning? We're not due to be at the school auditorium until 5:00 p.m. The play starts at six thirty."

"Oh, don't be lazy, Kira," I scolded, shaking off my covers and getting out of bed. "It's scientifically proven that being an early bird helps you to be more active and successful throughout the day."

"Save your genius for the tourna—I mean, play. You'll need it to remember your lines," Kira added hastily. Good thing she caught herself. Mom was still in the room, and obviously, she had no idea that I was going to compete in the trivia tournament.

We dragged ourselves (or should I say, I dragged Kira) down the stairs and into the kitchen where a bowl of cereal was waiting patiently for us on the table. My dad sipped his coffee from the kitchen counter and gave us a warm smile as we ventured in. "It's the big day, girls!"

Kira rolled her eyes, but I knew that she was secretly bursting at the seams excited. I was too! I couldn't believe I had ever despised drama club like I had a few months ago. Now it was all I could think about.

Kira was shoveling her Cheerios into her mouth like one of those big pieces of machinery you see at construction sites. I found myself doing the same; my hand shook with every spoonful. I chalked it up to nerves.

As soon as I'd finished my breakfast, I grabbed my cell phone and started to dial Vera's number. I paused before hitting the green call button. It was only a quarter till seven, and Vera probably wouldn't appreciate being awoken at the crack of dawn by her ringtone. But just as I was about to turn my phone off, a call came through with her name on it! How ironic.

I jammed my thumb into the accept button and held my phone to my ear. Vera's voice bubbled through excitedly.

"Can you believe it?" she squealed. "It's finally here! The musical! And you're the star!"

I smiled so widely that it almost cracked my face in half. "I know! I know! I can't breathe. I can't wait."

"Me too! And by the way, if you need any help with the twin-switch thing, just let me know. I'll be backstage. We can go into the costume closet or something so nobody sees you and Kira swapping costumes."

"Perfect," I said. "Everything is running smoothly."

"Good luck at the tournament! You'll win, I bet. Prove that stupid Eleanore wrong!"

"You bet!"

We chitchatted at a rapid-fire pace for a while longer before I hung up and wandered into the living room. I found Kira sprawled on the sofa, staring unblinkingly at the wall clock.

"Watched pots never boil," I warned her before sitting down to observe the ticking hands as well.

"It's only seven o'clock," Kira griped. "No way can I last until five."

"You'll live," I said, though I felt just as impatient. "Five o'clock will come."

And come it did, after almost a full day of Kira breathlessly going over her lines and me privately studying my flashcards in my room, it was time to get to school so we could prep before the show. We practically burst out the front door, quickly telling our parents to be in the audience by six fifteen and to make sure to wave!

Walking to school on a Saturday felt weird, and walking without a backpack felt even weirder. By nature, we weren't actually *walking*, more like sprinting.

"Gotta...make it...to school," Kira puffed, suffocating as we ran.

"We'll be on time," I managed.

CHAPTER 23

Kira

Katelyn and I arrived at Pine Hills winded and out of breath. We had left the house wearing very similar outfits so that it would be harder for people like Mrs. Kerrington to know who's whom. (I thought this was a clever move on our parts.)

Katelyn swung open the double doors, and together, we made our way down the hall to the auditorium. The school seemed so weird and mysterious on a Saturday—empty like a ghost town. There were no harried students speed walking to their next classes, and the lights seemed to be only half on. I shivered, even though I wasn't cold.

We turned a corner, and jolly Mrs. Kerrington awaited us at the auditorium doors. Her eyes seemed to be glimmering with excitement and anticipation. She scribbled our names off an attendance sheet and beamed.

"Ah! Kira and Katelyn. Our Wendy! And"—she frowned a little as if trying to remember something—"oh yes! And our Pirate #6. That's right."

I tried not to feel hurt that Mrs. Kerrington had forgotten my role. I replied cheerfully, "Yep, that's us! Where should we go?"

She beckoned us into the auditorium where every square inch of space was occupied by students frenziedly rehearsing their lines one last time. Yumiko and several others paced around with their scripts in hand, chanting words over and over like a poem. I thought sour Yumiko had a lot of nerve to be showing up here as a replacement for Wendy, even though it was clear that, at this point, we didn't need one.

A few girls and boys were sprawled on the floor with their eyes closed, trying to calm their nerves. There was a lot of "fanning with scripts" and "chugging water," and my heart skipped a beat just watching all the action. But Vera Smith, at the very back of the vast room, was the only one who didn't seem to be nervous. She was making herself busy unfolding chairs and lining them up in rows. The stage curtains were open, and behind them I saw Abby and the rest of the crew dashing this way and that, carrying crates and props and all sorts of bits and pieces. Lights flickered as a tall boy punched buttons on a control panel and shoved wires into place.

All in all, it looked like a dream come true.

Beside me, Katelyn started taking these massive deep breaths, and I tried to send her a telepathic message like, *Don't throw up!* I really hoped my sister could pull through for the second act and that stage fright wouldn't get the better of her.

Mrs. Kerrington interrupted my waterfall of emotions. "Well, girls, why don't you go in? Make yourselves at home. Rehearse, help set up chairs, whatever."

We obliged, and I led Katelyn over to where Vera was working. I had to step over quite a few stray scripts on my way.

"Hey, Vera." I tapped her on the shoulder, and she spun around eagerly.

Her eyes widened at the sight of us, and she started babbling at a mile per minute. "Kira! Katelyn! I can't believe today's the day! Do you think we can do it? I'm pretty sure the performance will be great, but what if I forget a line? What if I fall?" She waved her hands around madly.

I laughed. "We'll be fine, Vera. But look at the props and the backdrops! Aren't they *dazzling*?"

Vera looked over at the stage where the crew was still running around and setting up. "No kidding! Abby has done such a good job."

I grinned. "She's really good with that paintbrush."

Vera looked over at my twin who was standing silent and motionless beside me. Her eyes gazed off into space. "Katelyn, you're being awfully quiet. Anything on your mind?" asked Vera.

Katelyn was tensed and glanced around apprehensively before lowering her voice. "It's just…the switch. I'm scared."

"Don't be," Vera said automatically. "It will run smoothly. And if anything goes wrong, I'll cover for you."

I laid a hand on her shoulder and shook my head. "This is up to us. You really don't need to—"

"I'm here to help," she insisted, and I smiled in spite of the stress.

"You're going to do great," I assured Katelyn. "In the trivia tournament *and* the play."

My sister smiled, still distant. Her eyes seemed to have been glazed over with ice, and I was just starting to get seriously worried when she snapped out of it. "Speaking of the tournament," she said, straightening herself, "I'd better get going. It starts soon."

With that, she swiveled on her heel and dashed off in the opposite direction. Vera and I watched her dodge and leap over our cast-mates like a squirrel, apparently attempting to be inconspicuous but failing miserably. Then while Mrs. Kerrington had her back turned to help another student, Katelyn sprinted out the auditorium door and ran back down the corridor. The door shut behind her, and nobody even looked up from their scripts.

I heaved a sigh of relief. "Well, she got out safely. That means the first part of our plan is working."

Vera chewed her lip. "Do you think she'll be able to control her nerves? This is a lot for her. The tournament, the play, the switch."

I gulped. "I really hope so. Sometimes, when I think she's just gotten over her agitation, it just returns. Do you think it'll come back to bite her while she's performing?"

"I would hope not, but I guess we won't know until it's time."

Coincidentally, Mrs. Kerrington strolled up to us at this exact moment and boomed, "It's five fifty—it's time! Everyone has to move, move, move out of the main area. We'll be lowering the lights soon as parents will begin arriving in about twenty-five minutes.

Vera, you should put your Tinker Bell dress on. Katelyn, you should go get your Wendy costume. It's hanging up in the dressing room backstage."

I stared at her. Did she not notice that Katelyn wasn't with us? Then with a shock, I realized she was speaking to *me*. Somehow, she thought I was my sister and didn't question it at all! She hadn't even remembered to ask "Kira" to get into *her* costume. There she goes, forgetting me again. At least her short memory works better for our plan. I guess that's one of the benefits of having a tiny part in the play.

"Well?" Mrs. Kerrington demanded, tapping her wristwatch. I could see she was already getting impatient with the musical beginning so soon. "Are you going or not?"

I snapped out of my trance like a light switch and nodded feverishly. "Let's go, Vera. Backstage it is."

Vera looked at me with wide eyes, and we both bounded off toward the dressing room. Behind us, I heard Mrs. Kerrington moving on to another group, giving them the same instructions.

Vera and I climbed the steps up to the stage where we were met by a crew member who was helping to direct flustered students around. He had a clipboard in one hand and a walkie-talkie in the other. Wordlessly, he pointed a finger at a door behind him that was labeled Dressing Room. I thanked him before racing off.

We flung open the door and stepped into a room about the size of a kitchen. There were benches in the center, and the walls were covered floor to ceiling in cubbyholes. Some of the cubbyholes contained wigs, shoes, and makeup, among other random costume-related items. The whole room smelled strongly of hairspray, and it felt like I was really behind the scenes on Broadway. I wanted to stand there forever and let the feeling sink in.

Then I saw the green dress, brown-and-red tunic, and the blue silk nightgown hanging delicately in the corner.

CHAPTER 24

Somehow, I'd managed to escape the auditorium, unseen by Mrs. Kerrington and the other students. I silently traversed the halls, praying that Mr. Clark or some other teacher wouldn't come cruising around a corner. I'd have a lot of explaining to do if *that* happened.

I arrived safely at the gymnasium before the trivia tournament began at six o'clock. I signed myself in at the table beside the door and then quietly slipped inside. The gym seemed to be more alive than I'd ever seen it: parents chattered excitedly among themselves from the bleachers; competitors were selecting a seat from the chairs lined up in the very center of the court; and the three elderly judges sat primly at a table, shuffling and going over papers.

My heart began to pound, and my hands felt clammy. I counted twenty-four other competitors in total. I'd have to defeat twenty-three of them to make it to the finals where I'd be pitted head-to-head against one worthy opponent who would most likely be prissy Eleanore. I could see her now, seated with her legs crossed on one of the center chairs. I swallowed my cowardice and drew forward to select a chair of my own.

Unfortunately, I'd spent so much time dillydallying and observing that every last seat had already been taken except for the one directly next to my sour-mouthed nightmare Eleanore. I had no choice but to sit there.

Eleanore narrowed her eyes at me as I took my place. "What are you doing here, Katrina? Aren't you supposed to be in the *auditorium* for the *musical*?"

"It's *Katelyn*," I hissed. "And...and I quit the play." I tried to think fast. "Yumiko is taking my place. She's my understudy, you know."

Eleanore sniffed. "Happy to see you've made the academic decision of attending the tournament. It's *much* more sophisticated than prancing around on a stage. Isn't it?"

This was beginning to get weird. Eleanore always toyed with satire, but I felt like she was going a bit overboard—*too* overboard. She spoke like she knew something I didn't.

I hesitated before answering. "Well, if you feel that way, all the better to you." Then to rub it in a little, I added, "I'll win this competition. Don't underestimate me."

"Sorry, Kallie," Eleanore said, "but I'd be surprised if you managed to win, especially since you just *quit the musical*."

I searched for the words to make some smart-mouthed comeback to her statement, but that last sentence confused me so much that I just sat there dumbfounded. Why did Eleanore suddenly care about the musical so much? Was it some tactic to knock me off my game? I wanted to ponder it more, but suddenly the gym lights dimmed dramatically.

A spotlight flickered on to illuminate the court. I felt all the eyes of the folks sitting on the bleachers aimed mercilessly at me—and the twenty-four other contestants—in our chairs in the center of the floor. I fidgeted nervously and remembered that my parents were probably getting seated in the auditorium right at this moment, preparing to watch my twin sister pretend to be me in *Peter Pan*.

Our school principal, Dr. Evans, stepped tentatively up to the podium in front of the judges' table. He took out a crumpled sheet of paper from the pocket of his tweed jacket and held it up before him, fussily adjusting his reading glasses.

"Good evening, Pine Hills," he said gruffly into the microphone. "I am Principal Evans, and I'm pleased to commence this year's trivia tournament. For the duration of this competition, I will be the sole employee reading off questions to our clever students here. The judges will only interrupt if they feel it is necessary to."

He paused to flip a page of the crumpled paper packet he was holding. "I will now explain the way that this competition will work. It will begin with an indefinite series of preliminary rounds, which will only conclude once there are two students remaining. Each round will be assigned a theme, and every question asked during this round will relate to said theme. Students will stand up when it is their turn to be asked a question. If they answer correctly, they will remain in the tournament. If they answer incorrectly, they will be eliminated and shall take a seat up in the bleachers to spectate the remainder of the competition. Once we are down to the final two contestants, they will go head-to-head in a rapid-fire quiz round in which the student who answers the most questions correctly will be crowned our school champion."

The audience roared with applause whilst we, the competitors, glanced anxiously around the room. The trivia tournament was about to begin, and I could hardly keep in my excitement. This was everything I'd worked for, everything I'd waited for, and it all boiled down to tonight.

"Without further ado, we shall start round one," said Dr. Evans. "The theme of this round is geography."

I cheered inwardly. Geography was one of my best subjects.

"May our first contestant, Gemma Robertson, rise?"

Gemma was a lanky girl who happened to be seated farthest to the right in our row of chairs, which gave her the intimidating role of being first for every round. She appeared to be so ready for her question that she knocked her chair over in a rush to stand up. Uncomfortable murmurs and coughs flew across the room as she set it back upright, and I thanked my lucky stars that I wasn't the one having to face that embarrassment. "I'm ready," she said, her cheeks bright pink.

Dr. Evans daintily picked up a card from a small stack he had set before him and cleared his throat. "Gemma, your question is, What is the official language of Brazil?"

Gemma stared down at her toes sullenly and thought for a moment before answering. "Spanish?" she said hopefully.

I cringed. I knew she was wrong even before Dr. Evans said it.

"I'm afraid that is incorrect," he declared, and I watched Gemma visibly shrink. "The correct answer was Portuguese. You may take a seat at one of the bleachers."

One of the judges scratched something off a score sheet. Gemma dragged herself miserably over to where the audience members were seated. She got a few polite claps, but I remained motionless. This was a contest, and so far, we had one down, twenty-three to go. I was trying my best to focus and root myself at the moment, but I could feel myself drifting off into a fantasy where I was holding up that trophy for Eleanore Anderson to see.

"Next," said Dr. Evans, "we have Jeffrey Curtis."

The boy of the corresponding name rose from his seat and clasped his hands in anticipation of the question.

Dr. Evans read off another card. "Jeffrey, your question is, How many countries border Latvia?"

Jeffrey shut his eyes and counted on his fingers, muttering something unintelligible. After about ten seconds, he reopened his eyes. "Four," he said confidently.

"That is correct," Dr. Evans said. "You may sit back down. Eleanore Anderson, you are our next contestant."

Eleanore was up, which meant it'd be my turn next. The thought gave me a rush of panic and adrenaline. I'd have one shot to get my question right, and if I didn't, I was done. That couldn't happen. I *had* to beat Eleanore. My adversary stood up, preparing for her question.

"Eleanore, your question is," dictated Dr. Evans, "The city of Baghdad lies along what river?"

Eleanore gulped and chewed her lip, and for one blissful moment, I truly believed she was stumped. But no, of course, she answered, "The Tigris River," with accuracy and was rewarded with unfaltering applause.

And then it was Katelyn Dorsey's turn.

CHAPTER 24

Kira

"It's gorgeous!" I exclaimed, twirling in my blue dress. The silk billowed in waves around me like it was floating on clouds.

Vera and I had both quickly shimmied into our costumes and were now admiring ourselves in the dressing room mirror. The brown-and-red tunic was still untouched on its hanger; that would've been for the pirate role assigned to the real Kira Dorsey in the second act. I'd have to rush back and put it on once I assumed my true identity, but at the moment, I was Katelyn, and I only needed Wendy's blue dress.

Vera wore Tinker Bell's green dress and tiny blue wings made of foam. "Aren't our costumes great? Gotta thank the seamstresses on our way out."

I twirled again. I wanted to spend more time marveling at myself in the mirror, but a crisp knock at the dressing room door interrupted my fashion show.

Mrs. Kerrington's head popped out from the crack in the door. "Are you girls finished? We're waiting for you. The audience has been seated, and the curtains will rise in fifteen minutes."

"Yes, Mrs. Kerrington," Vera and I chimed in unison.

"Come along," she said briskly, ushering us out the door. "Abigail will take you from here."

I felt someone grab my arm and yank me into a small area behind the stage; it was so dark that I could barely make out who it was. But my eyes adjusted quickly, and I could make out the smiling form of my best friend, Abby.

"Hey, Vera. Hey, *Katelyn*," she said, a mischievous glint in her eye. Vera giggled softly, but I tried to swallow my laughter. It was game time, and I needed to be serious. Still, it was hard to focus when there were dozens of techies and actors that were bustling this way and that around me. Shadowy figures were speaking in hushed whispers while fixing lights, unraveling wires, and adjusting their costumes. It was overwhelming and breathtaking at the same time.

I cleared my clouded mind. "Is everything running smoothly? The props, the tech stuff?" I asked Abby.

She nodded. "Do you feel ready? The show will be starting soon. I saw your parents in the audience."

I felt a pang as I realized that Katelyn's trivia tournament would be in full swing by now, and both of my parents were here—watching *me* pretend to be *her*.

Vera nudged me. "Just to recap, you're doing the first act, then Katelyn will run over and swap with you? And you'll get ready for your pirate?"

"That's the goal, yes."

"Do you have all of your lines, songs, and choreography memorized?" Vera scrunched up her eyebrows. "You're going to be the lead. You'll have to say monologues, sing Katelyn's solo. I know you'll be great, but I just want you to feel ready."

"Luckily, hours of practicing have prepared me," I stated proudly. "I'll do well. I know I will."

"That's the attitude!" Abby grinned. "Anyway, let's quit the talking and get you two ready."

Like clockwork, Jacob Thompson materialized in front of us. "All right, costars, word is that the curtain goes up in five. Vera, did you remember to sign in at the auditorium doors?"

Vera rolled her eyes. "Yes. I'm not *that* forgetful."

Jacob turned to me. "Don't let stage fright get the better of you, okay, Katelyn?"

My eyes bugged, and I choked out an affirming response. *Remember: Jacob doesn't know that you're actually Kira.* It was so hard to juggle the people that knew who I was, and the people who were convinced I was my sister.

Abby clapped her hands, interrupting the awkwardness. "Let's get moving!"

She guided us through the throngs of actors down to the wings, and I could feel the adrenaline start pumping. *This is your night. Enjoy it.*

"Look at me." Abby spun me around to face her and dusted off my costume from top to bottom. Then she put her hands on my shoulders. "You're gonna do great. Don't think about the switch. Think about being Wendy Darling."

I took a shaky breath. "Gotcha."

I felt an emotion I had never felt before—excitement mixed with fear mixed with nostalgia mixed with expectation. Vera squeezed my hand, and Jacob nodded encouragingly. I wanted to thank them, especially Abby and Vera, for everything. For keeping all my secrets regarding the switch. For standing behind me when I was scared.

A crew member shouted something from down the hall, and Abby started cranking a wall-bound handle. The lift lines above me started to move. The curtains began to rise. This was it!

The stage lights flickered on, almost blinding me. Mrs. Kerrington stepped onto the stage holding a microphone and waved enthusiastically at the audience. It was so dark that all I could make out were the silhouetted heads of watching parents.

Mrs. Kerrington got rounds of cheerful applause and brought the microphone to her mouth. "I want to start by saying thank you to everyone who has worked on this show. All the crew, all the cast, everyone has practiced so hard to put on this musical tonight. And a special congratulations and good luck to our stars, Jacob Thompson, Vera Smith, and Katelyn Dorsey."

The audience erupted with claps and cheers. *Kira, not Katelyn.*

Mrs. Kerrington smiled and continued, "Thanks to everyone who is sitting here in the audience. I'm sure you'll be emphatically impressed with what your children have produced. I won't hold you any longer. This is *Peter Pan*."

More claps, and the lights shut off briefly, flooding the room with darkness. Jacob and Vera shoved me forward. My feet seemed to have minds of their own; I soon found myself seated in the center of the stage on a prop bed across from the one Wendy's brothers were sprawled across. John and Michael were the names of the characters, but I didn't know the actors personally. It was so terribly dark.

The lights flickered on, the audience *oohed*, and I absorbed everything in half a second. Here I was planted on the stage, opening the musical. Jacob, Vera, and many other actors waited patiently in the wings to my left and right for their entrance. Directly in front of me was a sea of spectators, so vast I almost forgot my very first line.

I picked the prop book, carefully prepared in its place by the crew, up off the bedsheets. I sat crisscross applesauce and pretended to read to my brothers, John and Michael.

I opened the book. "Little Red Riding Hood, Goldilocks, which bedtime story would you two like for me to read tonight?"

"Jack and the Beanstalk!" Michael shouted enthusiastically.

At precisely the same time, John yelled, "The Tortoise and the Hare!"

They proceeded to tackle each other in an effort to have their story chosen. "You chose last time!"

"I want Jack!"

"That's a boring story!"

"Settle down," I croaked, trying to ignore the relentless attentive stares of the audience. I was Wendy, not Kira, not Katelyn. I had to root myself into the story of *Peter Pan*. "We'll read Cinderella. How about that?"

The two boys erupted in hollers of protest, and soon enough, our parents—George and Mary Darling—rushed into the scene from the wings. Mother wore an evening gown, shimmering with sequins. Father wore slacks and a crisp white shirt.

"Children!" Mother scolded. "You need to quiet down. It's late, and your father and I are to be leaving for a party. Wendy, *please* be a responsible big sister."

I put on my best insulted-but-also-obedient face. Father strode over and snatched the storybook out of my hands, snapping it closed.

"I think it's time to go to bed." He stared me dead in the eye, almost dragging me out of the fictional world of the Darlings. *Don't let go. You're Wendy. Don't let them stop you.*

"Father!" I shrieked.

"Father!" John and Michael screeched.

"That's quite enough," Father said stiffly. "It's time to sleep."

We, children, had no choice but to obey. Our parents ushered themselves off into the wings and backstage.

I tucked myself under the covers and shut my eyes, and I could hear my brothers doing the same. Then one of the soundtracks started to play—a curious and inquisitive melody of the flute.

I opened one eye. Jacob and Vera—I mean, Peter and Tinker Bell—entered here, almost tripping over themselves in their hurry. Tinker Bell crossed her arms and glared at my sleeping form. Peter rooted himself between the two beds and snapped his fingers.

I sprung straight up like the snap was a gunshot. Michael yelled, "It's a pixie!"

I knew I was supposed to say something, but I was speechless. I couldn't find the words. I was forgetting a line! Like a deer in the headlights, I sat there with a terrified expression on my face.

I met Jacob's eyes, and we made some unspoken internal connection. "It's…me. Peter Pan," he improvised. I knew that line was never in the original script.

"Peter Pan?" My voice shook.

"That's right," Peter said, and the tension was released. "Do you want to learn how to fly?"

Tinker Bell turned bright red and stormed right up to Peter. She shook her first in his face, and Peter shrunk back. I knew that Tinker Bell's character never spoke as she was a fairy, so she expressed herself through dramatic movements.

"Fly!" John and Michael yelled, leaping out of their beds. They raced across the stage and shoved Tink out of Peter's way. The two brothers bounced up and down like moles in Whac-A-Mole, peppering Peter with questions.

I daintily stepped out of bed and tiptoed toward the group of three boys. Tinker Bell had stormed off into a corner of the stage to sulk.

I took a deep breath. "Can you really teach us to fly?"

Peter winked. "You bet!"

Tinker Bell turned flaming red again (I really don't know how Vera does that on command) and scrunched up her face. She slumped in front of a prop bed, crossed her arms, and glared at me like I was the bubonic plague. She let out an obnoxiously loud noise of displeasure.

Jacob bounded over to her. "Come on, Tink. Let's teach them to fly."

CHAPTER 26

Katelyn

"Katelyn, your question is—" Dr. Evans mused as he plucked a note-card off the stack. He cleared his throat. "What is China's most populous city?"

Whew! How did I get such an easy question? Right away, I answered, "Shanghai."

"Correct," said Dr. Evans. I collapsed into my chair, relieved, ignoring the dirty looks Eleanore was giving me.

The minutes ticked by as the tournament's first round met its end, each competitor answering a single question. Some got theirs correct; others weren't so lucky. I tallied up those who'd been eliminated. Alicia Robertson, who'd been the first answerer, was one, plus the kids who'd come after me: LeeAnn, Matthew, Jada, Zack, Mia, Mason, and Holly. Quite the list, considering it had only been one round. That left sixteen remaining, exactly two-thirds of the original number of competitors. Jeffrey, Eleanore, Heather, Julia, Amar, Sebastian, Andrew, Pete, Lisa, William, Natalie, Tim, Augustine, Summer, Henry, Josiah, and I were all still fighting in the competition.

The second round commenced; mathematics was the category. Not my strongest suit, but I'd still be able to tackle it.

Despite my confidence, some of the questions my predecessors got asked were really, *really* hard for a bunch of sixth graders. Jeffrey Curtis's question was 206 multiplied by seven, a tough problem to do in your head. He stood there for a solid twenty seconds as Dr. Evans tapped his watch impatiently. Eventually, Jeffrey squeaked out, "One thousand, two hundred...and two?"

Nope. Dr. Evans sighed. "I'm afraid that's incorrect. The correct answer is one thousand four hundred and forty-two. You have been eliminated."

Jeffrey's face crumpled, and he walked sullenly over to the bleachers. I almost felt bad for him, except for the fact that it was one less competitor for me to deal with.

Eleanore's question was $7(108 \div 9)$, which she answered with ease faster than I could in my head. She sat down triumphantly after Dr. Evans confirmed her response as the correct one.

I stood up shakily. It took all of my will not to start hyperventilating, so I put my game face on to cover my nerves.

"Katelyn, your question is," said Dr. Evans. "What is four to the fifth power?"

I tried not to gasp aloud. Thank goodness! An easy question. Four times four was sixteen, duh, and sixteen times sixteen is two hundred and fifty-six. That made up four to the fourth power, but I needed four to the fifth power. So 256 multiplied by four equals 1,024, also known as the correct answer.

"One thousand and twenty-four," I said with a flourish.

"Good job, Katelyn. That is correct."

I felt like I was floating on clouds. The majority of the rest of the competition passed smoothly; I survived several more rounds with themes like spelling and ancient history. Others weren't so lucky. Heather, Julia, and Amar were eliminated during the spelling round. Pete, Lisa, William, and Natalie got kicked during ancient history. And lastly, we had an oddball round on Greek mythology in which six more kids were eliminated.

That left two.

"Eleanore Anderson and Katelyn Dorsey, you two are officially our finalists!" Dr. Evans announced. The audience applauded. The judges remained stoic and icy cold.

My brain couldn't quite process what was happening. I was a finalist? Against Eleanore? I was unable to tell if this was a blessing or a curse.

Dr. Evans coughed politely to reign the audience back into the competition. "I shall now explain the rules of the final round. This will be rapid-fire. Questions may pertain to any subject or category. I will ask each finalist five questions, alternating between the two of them, and whoever answers the most correctly out of five will be declared our winner."

I saw Eleanore glare at me out of the corner of my eye. I kept looking forward and ignored her.

Dr. Evans officially began the round with Eleanore's first question. She stood up, looking expectantly at the principal. He shuffled his flashcards once more and delicately selected one from the top of the deck. "Eleanore," he said, clearing his throat, "your question is, What is the official currency of Russia?"

"The Russian ruble," Eleanore answered without missing a beat. She plopped back into her seat, and it was my turn to stand up.

Dr. Evans asked, "Katelyn, what year was the nineteenth amendment passed?"

Simple history. I answered, "1920."

Eleanore's turn again. This seemed to be moving so quickly! "Eleanore, how long is an Olympic swimming pool?"

"Fifty meters long."

My turn. I stood up. "Katelyn, what is cynophobia?"

"The fear of dogs," I answered.

I sat down; Eleanore stood up. "Eleanore, who named the Pacific Ocean?"

"Francis Magellan."

I stood up. "Katelyn, the god Vishnu is recognized in what religion?"

I had to think about this one. "Hinduism."

Dr. Evans asked, "Eleanore, this is your fifth and final question. Who was the first female pilot to fly solo across the Atlantic Ocean?"

"Amelia Earhart," Eleanore responded.

"And lastly, Katelyn, your fifth and final question is"—Dr. Evans sniffed—"What was the first soft drink in space?"

"Coca-Cola," I said and collapsed into my seat. That was the end of the final round.

"The judges will now evaluate your responses and score you," Dr. Evans said. "Please give them a minute."

A minute felt like an eternity, and the entire gym held its breath in anticipation. I could hear my own jittery heartbeat, and I was sure the dozens of people in the bleachers could too.

I watched the prim-and-proper judges pore over score sheets, writing and erasing, and discussing with one another. One of the lady judges started blabbing rapidly to the judge next to her, and he quickly scribbled something in a notebook. Then the lady looked at me over her brown rimmed spectacles, and I fought the urge to look away. My fate was in their hands. I couldn't bear the suspense!

One of the judges waved Dr. Evans over from his podium. He joined them at their table, leaned over, and a judge whispered something in his ear. He then straightened up and returned to the podium.

"The judges have determined a winner," Dr. Evans said. The audience, and me, collectively gasped. Eleanore remained confidently in her seat, already certain she was going to win. I'd never been so sure of myself like she always seemed to be. I crossed my fingers and then my toes within my shoes for luck.

"Eleanore, Katelyn," said Dr. Evans, "both of you have done well in this extremely challenging tournament. However, Eleanore… Eleanore, the answer to your third question was *Ferdinand* Magellan, not Francis. That sets you at a score of four out of five. Katelyn Dorsey has come out on top with a score of five out of five answers correct, making her our winner for tonight!"

I screamed. I beamed. I leaped out of my seat. The audience started cheering and shouting and clapping, but all the chaos faded to murk as I skipped over to receive my plaque from Dr. Evans. He congratulated me warmly with a high five too for good measure. I smiled so wide that I thought my cheeks would crack in half.

All I'd ever wanted was coming true! I traced the golden inscribed letters of *Winner* on my beautiful plaque with my index finger. The wood felt cool to my touch. I wanted to linger in this moment forever, rejoicing in my victory while Eleanore sulked very unsportsmanlike in the corner.

I felt someone yank me aside by my arm; the spell was broken. I was led blindly toward the gymnasium doors by my captor. My head snapped up, my vision refocused—the person who'd splintered my ecstatic daydream was Kira's best friend, Abby. Upon seeing her anxious face, I glanced quickly at my wristwatch. It was 7:02 p.m. Not only was the trivia tournament over, but also the first act of the play was too!

"Katelyn, we've gotta go," Abby said urgently in a low voice. Strands were escaping from her tightly braided hair; she must've sprinted right from the auditorium to come get me. Her walkie-talkie was clasped so tightly in her hand that her knuckles were turning white. "It's already intermission."

I looked around helplessly and saw Eleanore whispering something to Dr. Evans off by the judges' table. *No!*

Dr. Evans looked around; his face hardened into a stern glare and then locked eyes directly with me. My heart turned to ice. I couldn't speak. I couldn't breathe. And Dr. Evans was walking toward me, almost in slow motion. *Eleanore did it! She told him about the twin switch!*

I was rooted to the spot, vaguely aware of Abby yanking me with all her might through the doors and out of the gym.

"Run, Katy, run!" Abby hissed in distress and impatience. "Give me your plaque, I'll hold it for you while you're on stage. We'll deal with Eleanore and Evans later. We've gotta get back to the auditorium *now.*"

I gulped.

We ran.

CHAPTER 27

Kira

"That was the best thing I've ever done!" I squealed, teary-eyed. "I miss it already!"

It was intermission, and I was just beyond the wings with Jacob and Vera. Abby had run off unexpectedly to fetch Katelyn to step in as Wendy, but I didn't *want* her to step in as Wendy. I was having the time of my life performing.

The curtains were closed. I could barely breathe. I'd sung Wendy's entire solo without messing up once! I hadn't forgotten a line of her monologue! I recalled the unfaltering cheers and claps at the end of each. The applause consumed me; I drank it up like hot cocoa, and I could still hear it ringing in my ears even now in the wings. *This* was what I wanted to do forever and ever—show business! I was on cloud nine.

I could hear the audience chattering enthusiastically about the play and how wonderful it'd been so far. I could almost imagine my parents raving about my, I mean, Katelyn's performance. From the wings, I saw a handful of crew members setting up props for the second and final act. Somebody wheeled a massive wooden ship (constructed by Abby, of course, our finest) right into the very front of a stage left wing where it would be ready to sail onto the stage. Backdrops were swapped out. Floors were swept clean.

In my head, I went over the plot of the next few scenes. This act would consist of Peter being captured by Captain Hook, Tinker Bell saving Peter from a time bomb, followed by the dramatically cho-reographed battle scene against the pirates. I was a pirate, of course, which meant I really should be getting into my costume. If only I could be Wendy forever.

"Katelyn. Earth to Katelyn?" Jacob was nudging me. I'd barely noticed. It was pretty unsettling, how he kept calling me by the wrong name. (Of course, it wasn't the wrong name to *him*.)

"What?" I said.

"Did you have fun out there? I know you were really scared. At the rehearsals and everything." He looked like he was remembering all the times my sister had been shell-shocked or frozen on stage. How embarrassing.

"You were marvelous, Katelyn!" Vera interjected. "Simply per-fect. How do you feel?"

"Over the moon. It was the best thing I've ever done," I gushed. "I wish I could do it again."

As soon as the words had flown out of my mouth, I wished they hadn't. I resisted the burning urge to clap my hand over my big fat mouth. Vera pursed her lips, eyes wide.

I wish I could do it again? Of course, I was going to do it again. I was Katelyn, and I was supposed to be doing the second act. Kira was not going to do the second act. In fact, Kira was not supposed to be doing any acts at all. My statement about *doing it again* made zero sense from Jacob's point of view.

Jacob looked rightfully bewildered. "What do you mean? We have the whole second act to get through."

"I, well, uh." Tongue-tied. I felt my cheeks getting hot. How was I going to explain this one?

The most flawless timing saved me from having to explain myself. Miraculously and terrifyingly, two ruffians slammed into me at full speed. I stumbled backward, rubbing my side, and glared at my antagonists. I wasn't angry for long, though, it was Abby and Katelyn!

The two girls looked like they'd been through a hurricane: drenched in sweat, hair flying all over the place, panting like dogs. They must've sprinted straight here from the auditorium.

"Kira!" Abby shrieked and grabbed me by my shoulders. "What are you doing? You're supposed to be in the dressing room. Katelyn needs your costume, *now*."

I stole a glance at Katelyn helplessly, but she appeared just as urgent. I gawked at my blue dress, flustered. "But...I want to do the second act!"

Vera shoved Abby and me apart. "We've gotta get moving."

Jacob stood apart, looking horrified. His eyes were saucers. "Katelyn? Kira? What's going on?"

He wasn't the only one staring. Dozens of crew and cast members had stopped dead in their tracks, unblinking, goggling at us like we were a freak show.

We wasted no time. Abby hauled our group, minus the confused Jacob, through the throngs of people, ignoring their aghast expressions. We barreled into the dressing room which, thankfully, was empty. Abby locked it tight behind us, jiggling the handle as a precaution.

She clapped her hands three times. Vera, Katelyn, and I stood at attention. I'd never seen Abby so fired up.

"All right, y'all," she declared. "We have to move, move, move if we want to pull this off. We've got seven minutes left of intermission. Vera, help Kira get the blue dress off. Kira, prepare the pirate costume. Katy, you know what to do."

We sprung into action, assembly line mode. With Vera's aid, I shimmied out of the Wendy costume. Somebody tossed it toward my sister who caught it deftly and started putting it on. I yanked my patiently awaiting pirate costume off its hanger. The costume had quite a few parts to it: a feathered pirate cap with shredded ribbon hanging off it, a decoratively torn-up brown-and-red tunic with a leather belt, and knee-high combat boots. I threw everything on as quickly as I could, fastening the hat on with a few pins here and there. Katelyn was wearing Wendy's dress and stockings.

"Two minutes," Abby shrieked.

We were ready to go. We burst through the door and dashed off to our respective places backstage. Katelyn as Wendy and Vera as Tinker Bell bolted over to the stage's right wings where Jacob was restlessly anticipating them. Abby followed closely behind, ready to raise the curtains again. I shoved past dozens of people to find my place among the pirates on the opposite side of the stage. There were about six of us swashbucklers total, plus the flamboyantly dressed Captain Hook. I got a lot of stares. Word had flown quickly about the little incident we'd had backstage: the crash between the phony Katelyn and the real Katelyn. Hopefully, we'd be able to survive the second act without being confronted about that *situation*.

The curtain began to rise, and I knew Abby was working her magic. Standing on my toes, I squinted into the audience through the feathered pirate heads in front of me. I mostly just saw a mass of shadowy bobbing faces like I had when I was on stage for the first act. No way was I going to be able to find my parents. Whatever.

I was about to return to my normal hyper-focused performance mode when I noticed two looming figures in the very corner of the auditorium. All the way at the back, the last row of chairs.

Oh no.

Differentiating all the shadow people in the audience was nearly impossible, but you just can't miss that unmistakable pixie haircut. Yes, indeed, one of the looming figures was Mrs. Kerrington. Of course, she'd be watching the play. I wouldn't have been so concerned about her standing there if there wasn't a six-foot-seven hulk of a man next to her. I knew there was only one person that could be.

Principal Evans.

The stage lights glared a little too bright.

Chapter 28

Katelyn

How inconsiderate, I didn't even get time to hyperventilate before Abby started cranking that stupid handle as the curtains began to ascend. *This is it. This is really happening.* Who would've known that an argument over a desk would lead me to a starring role in a play?

The backdrop that was currently on the stage displayed a turquoise lagoon; flecks of white paint gave the illusion of sunlight hitting the waters. Cardboard rocks were arbitrarily scattered across the sand, I mean, floor. The crew had really outdone themselves.

The curtains seemed to rise in slow motion. Vera patted me on the back in a way that was meant to be encouraging, I suppose, but it only intimidated me more. I was about to sing and dance and lead the entire second act of *Peter Pan*! Right after I'd won the trivia tournament. Why had I agreed to do this? My heart pounded, and every intake of breath felt like a bullet train had just whizzed past me.

My thoughts were all muddled. How was I to remember my lines? *I will forget.*

I trembled. Somebody nudged me forward. I was supposed to be making my entrance.

Abruptly, I found myself thrust under the luminous stage lights with Jacob. Where was Vera? Oh, right, she wasn't in this scene. *This scene. The backdrops. Your lines.* Oh no! I had to say the first line. I had the first line. What was the first line?

"It's beautiful," I said mechanically. "The lagoon."

Come on, Katelyn, put some emotion into it!

"Isn't it?" Jacob—Peter—sashayed around the rocks, grinning. "I've heard mermaids live down here."

"It's beautiful!" I laughed with glee. Wait, no. I just said that.

Jacob cocked his head, perplexed. *No. No.*

"I wish I could just stay here forever, at peace," I amended, twirling around in my Wendy dress. I even smiled a little. *Come on. You've worked too hard for this to ruin it.*

Birds sang. Pleasant music played. I'd reviewed the script enough to know what came next. It was the first song of the second act. I was going to do this! I was going to fix the mess I'd made of my first lines!

The words seemed to come out without me thinking about it too hard, and suddenly, everything else dissolved. Peter sang a line. I did too. I danced a little like how Mrs. Kerrington had taught me. It was a simple, sweet tune about how lovely the lagoon was and the mermaids and everything. I could barely believe that I, Katelyn Dorsey, was actually *singing* in front of a crowd!

I sang the last line, giving it all I had, and the music cut out sharply. An ear-piercing scream shattered the serenity like it was a wine glass. Jacob and I jumped. *Don't panic. It's all part of the show.*

Jacob looked around wildly, his face pale. "I think that was Tiger Lily."

"Tiger Lily?" I said, my voice strained.

"She must be in trouble!"

I spun in a circle, trying my best to look panicked (which was easy, given my current state). I called Tiger Lily's name, and that was when I saw him.

Dr. Evans stood at the very back of the auditorium, his arms folded menacingly. All the air sucked itself out of the room like it was a vacuum.

"Wendy!"

Everything seemed to slow down. My ears rang. I couldn't believe this was happening. I was going to get into so, so, so much trouble. Eleanore must've ratted me out and told the principal about Kira's and my grand scheme. It took all of my being not to collapse.

"*Wendy!*" More sharply this time. Jacob swung me around to face him. His eyes were stormy. "You have to—we have to save Tiger Lily!"

I nodded so hard that my head almost toppled off. I couldn't remember what I was supposed to say. "Yes. Let's go. Let's go."

He yanked me offstage by my wrist, and that was the end of the first scene. I could hear backdrops flipping and new actors entering the stage for their parts, but all I knew was that I'd botched things horribly after how well I'd sung that piece too.

I stumbled into Vera in the wings. I grabbed her, and tears pricked the back of my eyes, threatening to fall.

"I can't do this! He saw! He knows, and now I'm going to get expelled!" I blubbered. "I've ruined everything!"

"Hey, hey, hey!" Vera looked me square in the eyes. "It was fine. You didn't mess anything up by freezing. You looked scared, just like how Wendy was supposed to. Nobody noticed a thing, I promise."

"I don't mean that." I took a deep breath. "Dr. Evans is in the audience. He's after me."

I could almost see the light fade from Vera's eyes. "Oh. Oh."

I bit my lip. "Kira and I are in hot water."

"You don't know that. Maybe he's just come to watch the play for a bit," Vera said reassuringly, but it mostly seemed like she was trying to reassure herself.

"You and I both know that's not the reason," I choked out. I really didn't want to cause a scene.

Before I could process things, someone dragged me over to a corner away from Vera. "Hey! Stop that!" I yelped, smacking the arm that was pulling me.

The yanker, which turned out to be my *sister*, swiveled around after leading me behind a wall of crates and cardboard boxes. "Chill out. I saw him too. You're fine. Everything's fine."

"No, it's not!" I exclaimed.

Kira rolled her eyes. "It will be, as long as you don't freak out on stage again. Just power through the show. Or do I need to take over as Wendy again?"

I couldn't help but chuckle, even though I felt like crying. "No. Shouldn't you be over with the buccaneers preparing to go on stage?" I could hear music and singing wafting over from the stage. I tried to squint through the stacked crates, but it was so dark that I couldn't even see the wings from where I was standing.

"Nah," Kira said. "Tiger Lily and Peter have a few scenes with Captain Hook before the rest of the pirates need to be called on for the fight scene. You're in that too, you know. It's the big finale."

I tried to regain my dignity. "Okay. I think I'm all right now. You go back to your *buccaneers*."

Kira cracked a smile. "Break a leg. Let's finish the show on a high note."

We parted our separate ways. Even though I'd only spent a minute with my sister, she never failed to cheer me up.

Vera greeted me warmly back at the wings. "All better? Tiger Lily and Jacob are finishing up their bit. It's almost time to engage in combat."

My heart skipped a beat. "I'm ready. Let's do this."

The finale commenced with the chiming of bells. The fight was fantastic. The wooden ship was wheeled onto the stage, and the pirates (including Kira) poured out of its decks. Jacob feigned, saving Vera from the rubble as my "brothers" and I were captured and tied up to the mast of the ship by Captain Hook. Jacob slashed at Hook with his prop dagger. Kira leaped about and roared, "Argh!" Vera flitted around basically becoming a nuisance for the offending pirates. I screamed and floundered my arms a bit to fit in with all the madness.

"You'll never win, Hook!" Jacob whooped and feinted tossing the wounded captain overboard. Jacob looked like he was having the time of his life performing, and shockingly, I was too.

Jacob slashed our ropes, freeing John and Michael and me. The pirates retreated back into the decks of their ship, which magically sailed offstage. In reality, I knew that the pirates weren't really below deck at all; they were behind the boat, wheeling it into the wings. But I didn't let that spoil the mystifying illusion of it all. This really was one heck of a play!

Vera, Jacob, my brothers, and I all danced around merrily on the open stage, singing a final song. Vera tossed some concealed pixie dust—which was actually glitter by the way—in the air. For once, Tinker Bell didn't look so nasty!

With the help of Tink's pixie dust, the Darlings were transported away from Neverland and back to their nursery at home where each child climbed into bed, just the way they had been before Peter Pan had flown through their window. The stage lights darkened to pitch-black. I could hear the audience on their feet in thunderous applause, going wild, screaming, cheering, and laughing. *We've done it!* I thought. *We've really done it!*

CHAPTER 29

The cast and crew interlocked arms for a final bow through the deafening applause. Katelyn, Vera, and Jacob stood front and center. I was off to the far right, practically in the wings, but I guess that's what I get for being Pirate #6. Even though my part was small, I think my smile was the very biggest among the proud cast of *Peter Pan*.

I could finally see my mother and father. There they were in the very front row, radiating joy, clapping, and jumping up and down. The sight of them filled me with delight, and I tried to ignore the stony-faced Dr. Evans who was still at the back of the auditorium with his arms crossed.

I gazed sideways across the long line of bowing cast and crew and watched as the three stars stepped forward for a separate bow. The applause grew even louder. Katelyn looked like she was having the time of her life.

After an excessively long clap fest, not that I'm not complaining about it, Mrs. Kerrington escorted herself upon the stage to conclude the play in the same way that she'd introduced it.

After taking center stage, she wiped a coating of sweat from her brow. She waved to the crowd, appearing as relieved as ever that the musical had been performed successfully. "I am so indescribably proud of all my students here tonight!" she praised. "The acting, singing, and unseen but unforgettable work of the crew has made *Peter Pan* the best show *ever* put on here at Pine Hills."

Roaring cheers from the audience.

"Now if you'd excuse me," Mrs. Kerrington said, "our school principal, Dr. Evans, would like to step up here for a brief word."

My heart began to thump. I met Katelyn's fearful eyes across the row of castmates. *What on earth did Dr. Evans want to talk about?*

Like a figment of my worst nightmares, Dr. Evans sauntered over in his tweed jacket from the back end of the room. He climbed the stage stairs two at a time and took the microphone graciously from Mrs. Kerrington.

He stared out into the crowd, brooding, for what seemed like an eternity before opening his mouth. "I am impressed by the work of our students here tonight. However, there is, ah, a *situation* that needs to be addressed."

The audience gasped.

No. No. No.

"Tonight, the stars of *Peter Pan*—" He paused to glance over his shoulder at us briefly before turning back to the audience. "Yes. Jacob Thompson, Katelyn Dorsey, Vera Smith. All of which have done an outstanding job performing tonight. Be that as it may, I have been informed by another student—"

Eleanore. Traitor.

"That two students, in particular, have not been completely honest with us tonight."

Hushed whispers flew across the auditorium, their echoes ricocheting off the cinder block walls. I could see my parents' perplexed faces in the front row, their eyebrows all scrunched up, frowning slightly.

Here came the kicker. Dr. Evans said gruffly, "The child that is listed on the playbill to have acted as Wendy tonight was not truthfully the child portraying her...*in the first act.*"

I couldn't bear to look at my parents' faces. I knew they would be so, so disappointed. I stared at my toes, wishing I'd never proposed this stupid plot of a twin switch.

Dr. Evans continued, "Katelyn and Kira Dorsey, may you two please come and stand beside me at the front of the stage?"

My whole body quaked as I walked over. I still didn't take my eyes off my pirate boots, which I was still wearing for the final bows. I took my place next to the principal and felt the shadow of my sister do the same. You could've heard a pin drop.

Dr. Evans looked at me and then at Katelyn. "It has come to my knowledge that a plot was hatched between the, ah, twins. Earlier this evening, Katelyn, who was cast as Wendy, did not perform the first act of the show. While she was in the gym across the building competing in our annual trivia tournament, Kira, who was cast as a pirate if I'm not mistaken, took her place as Wendy. At the conclusion of the tournament, for which she has won first prize, Katelyn traveled back over to the auditorium. The girls proceeded to switch back to their assigned parts for the second act."

I fought the urge to look at my parents. It was too painful. I squeezed my eyes tight, willing that the tears wouldn't fall.

"I nor any members of the staff were aware of this scheme." Dr. Evans paused for an excruciating five seconds so that the audience, cast and crew, and my heartbroken parents could let what they'd just heard sink in.

My pirate boots sure looked pretty.

"I have been pondering for the past forty-five minutes what I should do about this situation," said Dr. Evans. He shrugged. "I could write these two off with a detention. I could confiscate Katelyn's tournament win, or I could remove Kira from drama club. After all, a student unlawfully gave another student their part in the musical so they could compete in a tournament. I am sure that there were many other children here tonight who also wanted to participate in both but rightly chose only one or the other."

He eyeballed the audience, then us, then our castmates behind us, challenging anyone to disagree. I folded my hands primly and prayed that nobody could tell how much I was shaking.

"Yet," Dr. Evans said, "while I do not condone this type of behavior, I cannot name any rules that condemn it. Contrary to popular belief"—he scanned the auditorium, his eyes glittering—"the school rulebook does not specify that twins who swap places should be punished to any degree. Therefore, I have made the compassionate decision to congratulate Kira and Katelyn Dorsey on their masterful plot, and I am not a compassionate principal."

A few laughs arose from the audience. I broke my eyes away from my feet and lifted my chin a little, in disbelief of what I was hearing. I watched Katelyn do precisely the same beside me.

A playful smile decorated Dr. Evans's lips. "After all, little harm was done, and no real rules were broken. Now, Mrs. Kerrington?"

Mrs. Kerrington stepped forward from her courteous spot at the edge of the stage. She was carrying a towering golden trophy with the words First Place inscribed at its base. Katelyn gasped. A few people clapped.

"Katelyn Dorsey, I present to you your first-place trophy. Your supreme and unconquered intelligence has won you the trivia tournament!" Mrs. Kerrington proclaimed, passing the trophy into Katelyn's quivering hands. I clasped my hands together in glee.

Dr. Evans wasn't finished yet. "And, Kira, congratulations on memorizing and executing *two* roles flawlessly!"

A smile spread on my sister's face, and I realized there was one on mine as well. I could finally bring myself to look my parents dead in the eyes. They were on their feet, applauding us, while simultaneously cackling with laughter! I couldn't believe what I was seeing. Somebody tackled me from behind, and then another, and then all of my friends in the cast and crew engulfed Katelyn and me in a tsunami of *oh my gosh*es and *great job*s. Abby hugged me so tight that I thought my arms were going to pop off. Jacob Thompson gave me a high five. Vera screamed and jumped up and down. "We did it! The plan worked! And you're not getting expelled!" she squealed.

I felt overwhelmed with all of the compassion around me, all the cheering and shouting. I could hardly believe that I *wasn't* getting expelled! And that Katelyn had won the tournament!

EPILOGUE

Katelyn

The hallways were just as they always were—lively, bustling, and chaotic. My locker was the same as it always was: four bare walls with a stack of textbooks teetering at the bottom. Gently, I set my trivia tournament first-place trophy upon the stack, and my locker suddenly didn't seem so bare anymore. I stepped back proudly and found that I wasn't the only one admiring my handiwork.

"Congratulations," Eleanore said begrudgingly, standing beside me. "That trophy really sparkles under these cheap hallway lights, huh?"

I laughed in spite of myself. "Maybe the drama club crew can rig us some new ones."

Eleanore smirked. "Sure."

It was the Monday after the tournament and musical stunt, and I could still feel the lingering adrenaline of competing and performing on stage.

"You did great in the tournament. Really," I said truthfully. "A worthy opponent."

"Hey, it's cool. I can't win everything." Eleanore lowered her voice suddenly. "Especially since I didn't cheat this time around."

"You'd better consider yourself lucky that Abby and I didn't rat you out about all your prior conned victories," I joked. "That was the deal, remember?"

Eleanore shifted uncomfortably and stared down at her shoes. "Yeah, I know. I really suck, don't I? Cheating, lying, not upholding my side of the bargain." She paused to take a deep breath. "I'm going to do better, I swear."

Wow. Coming forward like that must have taken some serious guts. "That's great, Eleanore."

"I guess so," she said. Then she paused. "I don't know why you're not mad at me. You should be."

I laughed a little. "Oh, I am mad. But I'm forgiving too. And charitable. And gracious. And every other synonym for 'kind.'"

Eleanore rolled her eyes. "Okay, Miss Full-of-Herself. Relax, I'm kidding."

"Don't worry, I can tell!"

The bell rang, signifying the beginning of first period. Eleanore hoisted her backpack over her shoulders, preparing for departure.

"Congratulations, Katelyn," Eleanore said again, and it occurred to me that she'd finally used my real name.

"You just said Katelyn! Not Kristina or something silly. Ha!" I teased.

Eleanore sauntered away. "Don't get used to it!" she called back.

My first period would be honors math class. I made up my mind to do something I've wanted to do for weeks: pay Mr. Clark a private visit and thank him for his right judgment. He was the one who compromised my detention and ended up making me altogether happier. He was the one who improved my previously nonexistent social life. He was the one who changed my mind about drama club. Surely, he deserved a thank you.

I swung by his desk as my classmates were getting seated. He set down his pen and looked up from his half-graded worksheets, a slow smile spreading across his face.

"Well, hi, Katelyn," said Mr. Clark. "What's up? I heard about the events of Saturday."

I took a deep breath. "I wanted to thank you. For everything. The fact that you made me go to the *Peter Pan* audition? That really changed my life."

Mr. Clark chuckled. "I'm glad you had a good time. Congrats on the tournament win!"

"Aww, thanks," I said.

Mr. Clark dug around in his desk for something. "You know, Abigail Kent? She dropped something off. She said to give it to you after class, but now's as good a time as any." He pulled out an envelope from the top drawer. My name was written on it in swirly letters.

I took the envelope from him, not taking my eyes off it as I ventured over to my own desk. I sat down and opened the thin covering, and six pieces of paper tumbled out of the pouch.

The largest one was a folded-up letter. It read:

> One thing about working for the stage crew meant that we had full control over the school's technology. That includes photography and videography. So I called up one of my friends, who was also in the crew, and asked him if he could take some candids with his camera to document our work on the play. Over the past couple of weeks, he's been snapping pics left and right. Some of the prints came in today. I thought you might like to have them.
>
> —Abby Kent, Kira's best friend (and hopefully one of yours now too)!

I flipped over the five other papers. It turned out that they weren't just random scraps but instead glossy four-by-six professionally printed photographs.

The first one showed me up on the stage on the audition day, nervously shooting my shot for Mrs. Darling. My hands were folded, my knees were knocking, and my mouth was half-open, probably reciting a line or something. If only I had known then which part I would actually end up playing. I stared at my face in the picture, which was tainted with fear and discomfort, and remembered how out of place I used to feel. Those emotions are no more.

The second photograph showed Jacob jabbing me in the ribs at that one unfortunate rehearsal in which I was supposed to sing for the first time but instead chickened out. Jacob looked annoyed, I looked terrified, and Vera looked a mix of sympathetic and amused. Looking back on the memory, it did seem pretty funny.

The third photograph depicted Katelyn and "Katelyn" slamming into each other backstage. Yep, that was when I'd just finished the tournament, sprinted down the hall, and came flying into the wings, knocking into Kira who was pretending to be me in Wendy's blue dress. I giggled when I saw our shocked faces and the open-mouthed ones of the kids surrounding us.

The fourth one was a photograph of me performing on stage during the second act fight scene finale. I was tethered to the mast of the Jolly Roger being threatened by Captain Hook himself as Jacob bounded around slashing at pirates. My hair was in my eyes, and my expression was frozen in a scream. I really did look like Wendy.

The fifth and final photograph showed all the cast and crew, plus Mrs. Kerrington and Principal Evans up on the stage. The frame was frozen at the moment my name had been cleared. Dr. Evans had congratulated me on my win and assured me that I wasn't in any trouble. There were so many kids jumping around in the photo that it became very blurry, but the one in-focus part at the center showed Vera engulfing me in a massive hug with Jacob, Abby, and Kira beside us. Our smiles were almost wide enough to crack our faces in half. I hugged the photo to my chest.

Sure, Jacob could be a little high and mighty at times, and Abby could be loud, and Kira was my annoying twin, but all of them had become so near and dear to my heart in our time spent rehearsing and performing together.

And Vera. Vera was the sweet, caring friend I'd always wanted. I thought back to all the times we'd hung out and talked and laughed. All those times I thought I couldn't make it through the play or I was scared or I just needed a little reassurance, Vera was there. She'd helped me gain confidence; come out of my shell; and best of all, defeat my stage fright.

About the Author

Sophia Campbell was born in the suburbs of Washington, DC, and currently lives in Potomac, Maryland, with her parents and younger brother. She has been an avid reader from a young age and writing stories for nearly as long. Her first full-length novel *Stage Fright* has been in development since she was eleven years old. Additionally, Sophia has been receiving ballet training since she was four years old and continues to perform on stage in theaters such as The Music Center at Strathmore and the John F. Kennedy Center for the Performing Arts in Washington. While a full-time middle school student, she is enrolled in the preprofessional ballet program with the CityDance Conservatory. Other interests include painting, academic contests, traveling, and music. Her Greek Cypriot and British heritage have taken her to places as far as Cyprus, Greece, and England. She has a passion for theatrical arts and live performance.

CPSIA information can be obtained
at www.ICGtesting.com
Printed in the USA
BVHW052228090722
641765BV00005B/111